Cambridge Elements ≡

Elements of Paleontology
edited by
Colin D. Sumrall
University of Tennessee

DISARTICULATION AND PRESERVATION OF FOSSIL ECHINODERMS: RECOGNITION OF ECOLOGICAL-TIME INFORMATION IN THE ECHINODERM FOSSIL RECORD

William I. Ausich
The Ohio State University

Paleontological
SOCIETY

CAMBRIDGE
UNIVERSITY PRESS

CAMBRIDGE
UNIVERSITY PRESS

University Printing House, Cambridge CB2 8BS, United Kingdom

One Liberty Plaza, 20th Floor, New York, NY 10006, USA

477 Williamstown Road, Port Melbourne, VIC 3207, Australia

314–321, 3rd Floor, Plot 3, Splendor Forum, Jasola District Centre, New Delhi – 110025, India

79 Anson Road, #06–04/06, Singapore 079906

Cambridge University Press is part of the University of Cambridge.

It furthers the University's mission by disseminating knowledge in the pursuit of education, learning, and research at the highest international levels of excellence.

www.cambridge.org
Information on this title: www.cambridge.org/9781108789806
DOI: 10.1017/9781108893374

First published 2021

A catalogue record for this publication is available from the British Library.

ISBN 978-1-108-78980-6 Paperback
ISSN 2517-780X (online)
ISSN 2517-7796 (print)

Disarticulation and Preservation of Fossil Echinoderms: Recognition of Ecological-Time Information in the Echinoderm Fossil Record

Elements of Paleontology

DOI: 10.1017/9781108893374
First published online: January 2021

William I. Ausich
The Ohio State University

Author for correspondence: William I. Ausich, ausich.1@osu.edu

Abstract: The history of life on Earth is largely reconstructed from time-averaged accumulations of fossils. A glimpse at ecologic-time attributes and processes is relatively rare. However, the time sensitivity and predictability of echinoderm disarticulation makes them model organisms to determine postmortem transportation and allows recognition of ecological-time data within paleocommunity accumulations. Unlike many other fossil groups, this has allowed research on many aspects of echinoderms and their paleocommunities, such as the distribution of soft tissues, assessment of the amount of fossil transportation prior to burial, determination of intraspecific variation, paleocommunity composition, estimation of relative abundance of taxa in paleocommunities, determination of attributes of niche differentiation, etc. Crinoids and echinoids have seen the greatest amount of taphonomic research, and the patterns present in these two groups can be used to develop a more thorough understanding of all echinoderm clades.

Keywords: Echinodermata, taphonomy, preservation, paleoecology, crinoid, echinoid, asteroid, ophiuroid

ISBNs: 9781108789806 (PB), 9781108893374 (OC)
ISSNs: 2517-780X (online), 2517-7796 (print)

Contents

1 Introduction

The multielement echinoderm skeleton disarticulates in a predictable progression, which renders echinoderms model organisms for taphonomic studies. Consequently, much has been written on this topic, including thorough reviews, such as Lewis (1980), Donovan (1991), Brett et al. (1997), and Ausich (2001). Rather than attempt another full review, this Element will concentrate on understanding the following questions: When you find a fossil echinoderm – from a complete, articulated specimen to completely disarticulated and abraded ossicles (Figures 1 and 2) – what do you see? What data are encapsulated in fossil echinoderm occurrences? Initial observation of skeletal material clarifies morphology, but what other data are preserved – biologic, ecologic, biostratinomic, and diagenetic? Are the fossils

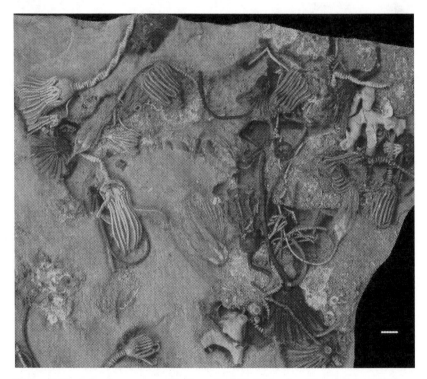

Figure 1 Buried paleocommunity from the Mississippian (Tournaisian) Maynes Creek Formation of Legrand, Iowa. Crinoids and blastoids occur together, and different species preserved characteristically in different colors: large white crinoid, *Elegantocrinus symmetricus*, large very dark crinoid *Cribanocrinus watersianus*, intermediate-colored crinoid in bottom center *Cusacrinus nodobrachiatus*, two very small cladids white, and white blastoids. (BC-173; scale bar 10 mm).

Figure 2 Fossiliferous bedding surfaces from Anticosti Island, Québec, Canada. **(1)** Mill Bay Member, Vauréal Formation, Ordovician (Katian) (OSU 54743). **(2)** Goéland Member, Menier Formation, Silurian (Aeronian) (OSU 54744) (scale bar 10 mm).

preserved where they lived or are they transported; if transported, how far? All echinoderm clades provide taphonomic information but because of their high relative abundance in the fossil record, the taphonomy of crinoids (e.g., Lewis, 1980; Donovan, 1991; Brett et al., 1997; Ausich, 2001; and Baumiller, 2003), and echinoids (e.g., Kier, 1977; Seilacher, 1979; Smith, 1984; Telford, 1985a, 1985b; Kidwell & Baumiller, 1990; Nebelsick, 1992, 1995a, 1995b, 1995c, 1996, 2008; Kroh & Nebelsick, 2003; Smith & Rader, 2009; Balaústegui et al., 2012; Mancousa & Nebelsick, 2013, 2015, 2017; Nebelsick et al., 2015; Grun et al., 2018; and Nebelsick & Mancosu, 2021) have been studied more extensively. The basic principles of these two clades are applicable for understanding the taphonomy of other echinoderm clades.

2 Echinoderm Skeleton

As noted, an echinoderm has a multielement mesodermal skeleton. Individual ossicles (skeletal plates) may be floating independently in mesodermal tissue (e.g., holothurians), imbricated (e.g., helicoplacoids, gogiids, edrioasteroids, ophiocistioids), or tessellate (abutting against one another). Tessellate plates abut one another in various configurations (Donovan, 1991); are bound together by either ligaments, muscles, or ligaments and muscles; or have interlocking stereom with varying degrees of strength. The strength of the bond between two plates by interlocking stereom is commonly correlated with plate thickness.

When secreted, the echinoderm skeleton is a high-magnesium calcite (see Gorzelak et al., 2012 and references therein). The magnesium content is variable and has been attributed to many causes (MacQueen et al., 1974; Gorzelak et al., 2012). Gorzelak et al. (2012) reported magnesium content between 1.83 and 3.55 wt.%. Variability existed between individuals as well as within a single ossicle, with higher concentrations in the center of ossicles (Weber, 1969; Stolarski et al., 2009; and discussion in Gorzelak et al., 2012).

Individual echinoderm ossicles have a stereom microstructure (Roux, 1970, 1974a, 1974b, 1975; Macurda & Meyer, 1975; Macurda et al., 1978; Smith, 1980) that is a porous arrangement of calcite trabeculae (Figure 3). When alive, space within the stereom was filled with mesodermal tissue. Each ossicle behaves optically as a single crystal of calcite despite the fact that each ossicle is a composite of nanograins (Gorzelak et al., 2016). Savarese et al. (1997) calculated the porosity of columnals in extant crinoids to range from 52–72%.

Echinoderm high-magnesium calcite is metastable, not in equilibrium with ambient conditions. Both the chemistry and stereom microstructure may be transformed during diagenesis as a function of local diagenetic conditions. Important diagenetic factors for echinoderm ossicle preservation include the following: primary magnesium content; porosity, permeability, and chemistry of the enclosing sediment; Eh, pH, and oxic chemistry of pore fluids; temperature, etc. (Gorzelak et al., 2016). Dickson (2001a) and Gorzelak et al. (2016) outlined several transformation pathways yielding different types of echinoderm ossicle preservation. Despite chemical and nanostructural changes, original single-crystal optical properties are typically maintained after occlusion of the original porosity during cementation. Dickson (1995, 2001a,

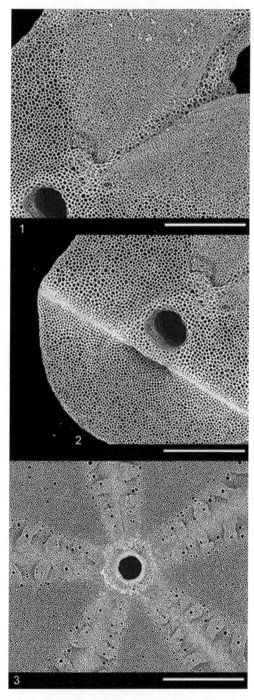

Figure 3 Stereom microstructure of the extant crinoid *Metacrinus* sp. **(1)** Upper portion of a brachial plate with axial canal to lower left and adoral groove to

Caption for Figure 3 (cont.)

upper right; ligamentary stereom to left an most of image muscular stereom (OSU 54740) (scale bar 500 μm). **(2)** Lower portion of a brachial plate with aboral ligament fossa beneath articular ridge and additional ligamentary fossae above articular ridge on either side of the adoral groove (OSU 54740) (scale bar 500 μm). **(3)** Central portion of a columnal with lumen in center of image, all ligamentary stereom (OSU 54739) (scale bar 1 mm). (SEM images taken by J. Sheets, Subsurface Energy Material Characterization and Analysis Laboratory (SEMCAL), School of Earth Sciences, Ohio State University.)

2001b, 2002, 2004, 2009) argued that the chemistry of well-preserved echinoderm calcite was correlated with ancient ocean Ca/Mg ratios; but Gorselak et al. (2016) argued that the echinoderm diagenesis system was too complex to reliably make this assumption.

3 Accumulations of Fossil Echinoderms

In shallow-water marine facies, echinoderms are among the more common bioclasts in many carbonate and siliciclastic settings. This was especially true during the Paleozoic, when crinoid bioclasts in rocks varied from seemingly random constituents (Figures 1 and 2) to beds comprised exclusively of crinoidal ossicles (Figure 4). Echinoderm-dominated beds include both allochthonous and autochthonous facies. Allochthonous facies range from thin to massive beds deposited by storms to areally extensive sediment gravity flows.

Within an autochthonous facies, individual fossils may be either autochthonous (preserved at the site where they lived) or parautochthonous (not preserved at their living site but fossilized within the sedimentary facies where they lived) (Kidwell et al., 1986). A typical autochthonous facies may contain a combination of autochthonous and parautochthonous individual fossils. Autochthonous echinoderm facies include a wide array of siliciclastic, carbonate, and mixed carbonate-siliciclastic depositional settings. Echinoderms may have been attached to a hard substratum during life. Hard substrata may be hardgrounds, shell pavements, or living organisms (Figures 5 and 6, Table 1). Rapid burial of both uncemented sessile or mobile organisms was varied and common. Such occurrences may contain only autochthonous organisms or a combination of autochthonous and parautochthonous organisms (Figures 7–10). A few examples are listed in Table 2.

Figure 4 Encrinite bedding surfaces. **(1)** Fort Payne Formation, Mississippian (early Viséan) of south-central Kentucky (OSU 54745). **(2)** Outcrop photograph of the Chicotte Formation, Silurian (Telychian) of Anticosti Island, Québec, Canada (scale bar 10 mm).

Through the Phanerozoic, suspension-feeding echinoderms were commonly associated with various types of carbonate buildups and were typically a dominant bioclast on buildup flanking beds. Examples include framework reefs, Waulsortian and other mudmounds, and other types of carbonate buildups, such as crinoidal packstone buildups (Figures 11 and 12, Table 3). Also, as discussed in the following, at certain times during the Paleozoic and Mesozoic, entire carbonate ramps were dominated by echinoderms yielding regional encrinites.

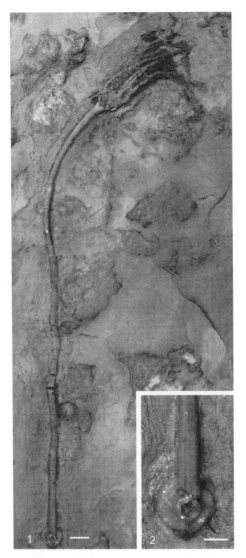

Figure 5 *Grenprisia billingsi* from the Bobcaygeon Formation of Ontario, Canada, Ordovician (Katian) (UMMP 74773). **(1)** Complete specimen (scale bar 10 mm); **(2)** Enlargement of holdfast cemented to a hardground (scale bar 5 mm).

4 Disarticulation of Echinoderm Clades

Under normal conditions, a dead echinoderm lying on the sea floor will typically disarticulate rapidly (e.g., Asteroids: Schäfer, 1972; Glynn, 1984; Moran, 1992. Crinoids: Blyth Caine, 1968; Meyer, 1971; Liddell, 1975; Baumiller, 2003. Echinoids: Schäfer, 1972; Smith, 1984; Greenstein, 1991; Nebelsick &

Figure 6 Six variously sized *Isorophus cincinnatiensis* and numerous
bryozoans competing for space on a *Rafinesquina alternata* brachiopod. From
the Florence, Kentucky, shell pavement, Correyville Member, Grant Lake
Formation, Ordovician (Katian) (see Shroat-Lewis, Sumrall et al., 2014;
photograph courtesy of C. D. Sumrall) (scale bar 5 mm).

Table 1 Examples of autochthonous attached
echinoderm paleocommunities buried on various
types of surfaces

Hardgrounds   .

              Brett & Liddell, 1978
              Koch & Strimple, 1968
              Guensburg & Sprinkle, 1994
              Sprinkle & Guensburg, 1995
              Sumrall, 2001
              Sumrall et al., 2001
              Cornell et al., 2003
              Brett et al., 2008

Shell pavements

              Bell, 1976
              Waddington, 1980

Table 1 (cont.)

	Meyer et al., 1981
	Kammer et al., 1987
	Meyer, 1990
	Sumrall, 2010
	Shroat-Lewis et al., 2011
	Shroat-Lewis et al., 2014
	Shroat-Lewis et al., 2019
Other biotic substrata	
	Guensburg, 1988
	Guensburg & Sprinkle, 1994
	Sprinkle & Guensburg, 1995
	Sumrall, 2000
	Sumrall et al., 2001
	Glass, 2005
Cobbles and Concretions	
	Sumrall et al., 2006

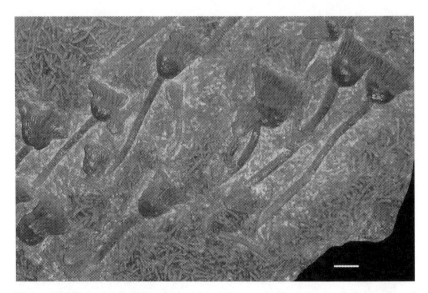

Figure 7 Aligned crinoid crowns with column attached. Large darker-colored crinoid, *Desmidocrinus pentadactylus*; smaller lighter-colored crinoid, *Carpocrinus* spp; small, abundant bioclast, *Coenites* (tablulate coral). See Franzén (1982) (RM Ec 27 500) (scale bar 20 mm).

Figure 8 Bed of *Glyptocrinus decadactylus* in various preservational postures, upper Fairview Formation, Ordovician (Katian), north-central Kentucky (CMCIP 50668) (see Milam et al., 2017) (scale bar 10 mm).

Figure 9 *Melonechinus* sp. from the St. Louis Limestone, Mississippian (Viséan) in Missouri. Field Museum of Natural History specimen (scale bar 20 mm).

Figure 10 Bedding surface with numerous *Archaeocidaris brownwoodensis* specimens and one crinoid (*Delocrinus* sp.) from the Winchell Formation, Pennsylvanian (Kasimovian), north-central Texas (see Schneider et al., 2005) (image courtesy of L. Boucher, Non-vertebrate Paleontology Laboratory, Jackson School Museum of the Earth, University of Texas at Austin) (TX) 000001967.100) (scale bar 20 mm).

Kamfer, 1994; Sadler & Lewis, 1996. Holothurians: Schäfer, 1972; Allison, 1990; Le Clare, 1993. Ophiuroids: Meyer, 1971; Schäfer, 1972.). Rapid disarticulation on the sea floor is also demonstrated by the relatively common fossil echinoderm occurrence of partial disarticulation of a specimen on a bedding surface. This includes parts of one individual preserved in close proximity, as well as specimens with the up-side partially collapsed but the down-side (in the sediment) still articulated. All things being equal, muscular tissue will decompose first; ligaments, the more refractive tissue, decompose next; and plates with interlocking stereom disarticulate last. Our understanding is based on both in situ observations (listed previously) and laboratory experiments (e.g., Asteroids: Schäfer, 1972; Allison, 1990. Crinoids: Baumiller, Llewellyn et al., 1995; Oji & Amemiya, 1998. Echinoids: Kidwell & Baumiller, 1990; Greenstein, 1991. Ophiuroids: Lewis, 1986).

Table 2 Examples of mobile or rooted echinoderm paleocommunities buried by an obrusion deposit

Asteroids

          Adkins, 1928
          Breton, 1997
          Blake et al., 2007
          Kühl et al., 2012
          Jagt et al., 2014

Asteroids and ophiuroids

          Rousseau et al., 2018

Blastozoans

          Ubaghs, 1963

Crinoids

          Laudon & Beane, 1937
          Lane, 1963
          Strimple & Moore, 1971
          Lane, 1973
          Meyer & Weaver, 1980
          Schumacher, 1986
          Ausich & Sevastopulo, 1994
          Taylor & Brett, 1996
          Brett & Taylor, 1997
          Gahn & Baumiller, 2004
          Kühl et al., 2012
          Brett et al., 2008
          Hagdorn et al., 2018

Crinoids and echinoids

          Hagdorn & Schulz, 1996

Echinoids

          Rosenkranz, 1971
          Schneider et al., 2005
          Smith et al., 2009

Echinoids and ophiuroids

          Tetreault, 1995

Gogiids

          Parsley & Zhao, 2006
          Lin et al., 2008
          Zhao et al., 2008
          Parsley, 2009
          Zamora et al., 2009

Table 2 (cont.)

Ophiuroids	
	Kesling & Le Vasseur, 1971
	Goldring & Stephenson, 1972
	Aronson & Blake, 1997
	Kühl et al., 2012
Ophiuroids and stylophorans	
	Reid et al., 2015

Figure 11 Cross section of bedding along an encrinite flank bed of the Waulsortian mudmound at Hanging Tor, Mississippian (Tournaisian), Pembrokeshire, United Kingdom (scale bar 10 mm).

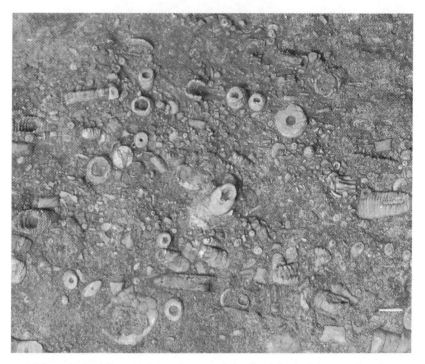

Figure 12 Bedding surface of an encrinite flank bed of the Waulsortian mudmound at Hanging Tor, Mississippian (Tournaisian), Pembrokeshire, United Kingdom (scale bar 10 mm).

In addition to this predictable sequence of tissue decay, varying aspects of constructional morphology impose constraints such that different echinoderm clades have characteristic styles of disarticulation. Susceptibility to disarticulation can be a defining characteristic of a class-level clade or may vary among clades within a class (Brett, et al. 1997).

If holothurians are included in the taphonomic grade scheme of Brett et al. (1997), a fourth grade should be added, as holothurian ossicles are scattered throughout the mesodermal tissue and can only be preserved in life association if the entire organism is preserved with soft-tissue preservation (Table 4) (Pawson, 1980; Sroka, 1988; Smith & Gallemí, 1991; Sroka & Blake, 1997). Individual holothurian ossicles, and more rarely clusters of ossicles, are recoverable from washed residues of unconsolidated sediment.

Ophiuroid and asteroid plates are typically not interlocked together so, in this case, whole animal disarticulation generally occurs at a pace equal to tissue decay. Thus, asteroid and ophiuroid mass fossil occurrences must be an example of rapid burial (Figures 13 and 14). Ophiuroids have been reported to

Table 3 Examples of carbonate buildups with flank beds dominated by crinoids

Framework Reefs	
	Lowenstam, 1957
	Wilson, 1975
	Brett, 1985
	Brett, 1995
Crinoid packstone buildups	
	Carozzi and Soderman, 1962
	Ausich & Lane, 1980
	Ausich & Meyer, 1990
	Meyer & Ausich, 2019
Carbonate mudstone buildups	
	Wilson, 1975
	Bridges et al., 1995
	Jackson & De Keyser, 1984
	Ausich & Meyer, 1990
	Lees & Miller, 1995
	Meyer et al., 1995

disarticulate much more rapidly than asteroids (Schäfer, 1972) and disarticulation rate among asteroid clades is a function of plate size and robustness (Allison, 1990; Breton, 1997). Consideration of the full range of constructional morphology motifs among Phanerozoic asteroids should reveal numerous asteroid taphonomic grades.

Echinoid spines (attached to the test with muscles) disarticulate and become disassociated from their test rapidly (Figure 10) (Aslin, 1968; Schäfer, 1972; Smith, 1984; Kidwell & Baumiller, 1990; Nebelsick, 1995b, 2008; Kroh & Nebelsick, 2003; Balaústegui et al., 2012; Mancousa & Nebelsick, 2013, 2015, 2017; Grun et al., 2018; and Nebelsick & Mancosu, this volume). Disarticulation of the echinoid test is a function of the degree of interlocking stereom between plates (e.g., Kier, 1977; Régis, 1977; Schäfer, 1972; Smith, 1984; Kidwell & Baumiller, 1990; Mancousa & Nebelsick, 2013, 2015, 2017; Grun et al., 2018; and Nebelsick & Mancosu, this volume). Among living echinoids, the strength of the connection between two plates is probably correlative with plate thickness in most cases, but exceptions exist. If Paleozoic forms such as the Lepidesthidae and *Melonechinus* are included, echinoid constructional morphology through the Phanerozoic has an even wider range of taphonomic grades within the echinoid clade.

Table 4 Modified, first-order classification of echinoderm preservational grades (modified from Brett et al., 1997). See Neblesick & Mancosu (this volume) for a thorough discussion of differential preservation potentials among echinoids

Category	Definition	Echinoderm Clades	Taphonomic Grades			
			A	B	C	D
Type 0	Ossicles not connected; scattered within mesodermal tissue	Holothurians	Rare: Entire body	Ossicles	Ossicles	Ossicles
Type 1	Ossicles loosely connected; rapid decay and disarticulation	Asteroids, cyclocystoids, edrioasteroids, gogiids, helicoplacoids, homalozoans, ophiocistioids, ophiuroids, some echinoids (e.g., echinothuroids), somasteroids	Rare: Entire body	Very Rare: Arms, Ossicles	Ossicles	Common: Ossicles
Type 2	Skeleton with loosely and more securely connected plates (tests, calyxes, pluricolumnals)	Most crinoids, most blastozoans, some echinoids (most regular and some irregular)	Rare: Entire body	Common: Calyx, Test	Common: Calyx, Test	Very common: Ossicles
Type 3	Dominant skeleton portions rigidly sutured (tests, calyxes, thecae)	Blastoids, some crinoids, irregular some irregular echinoids (clypeasteroids)	Relatively common: Entire body	Very Common: Calyx, theca, test	Common: Theca, calyx, theca, test	Rare: Test, thecae fragments

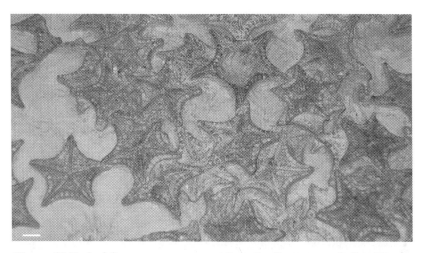

Figure 13 Bed of *Crateraster mccarteri* from the Cretaceous chalk of Travis County, Texas (scale bar 10 mm).

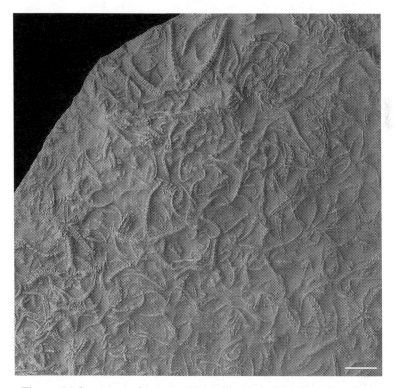

Figure 14 *Strataster ohioensis*, Meadville Shale Member, Cuyahoga Formation, Mississippian (Tournaisian, Ohio). Specimen lightly coated with ammonium chloride OSU 37312 (scale bar 0.5 mm).

The distinct contrast in constructional morphology in epifaunal versus infaunal echinoids is responsible for a strong taphonomic bias for irregular echinoids preserved as fossils during the post-Paleozoic (Kier, 1977; Régis, 1977; Smith, 1980, 1984; Kidwell & Baumiller, 1990; Greenstein, 1990, 1991, 1992; Nebelsick, 2013, 2015, 2017; Grun et al., 2018; and Nebelsick & Mancosu, this volume). For example, Greenstein (1990) recognized that in a contemporary setting, the ecological abundance of regular versus irregular echinoid abundance in sediment (as opposed to living communities) was heavily biased toward irregular echinoids.

Similar to echinoids, different crinoid clades disarticulated with definable similarities and differences. In general, if present, muscular articulations in arms were the first sutures to disarticulate, followed by ligamentary articulations between brachials, columnals, and calyx plates (note that Meyer & Meyer (1986) and Baumiller (2003) documented different orders of disarticulation among feather stars). As discussed in more detail in the following, the column first disarticulates in segments of pluricolumnals (broken sticks) (Baumiller & Ausich, 1992). Articulations with interlocking stereom disarticulate last with thinner plates commonly disarticulating prior to thicker plates (Meyer et al., 1990; Baumiller, 2003; Brett et al., 1997). Based on comparative taphonomic studies (Meyer et al., 1990; Brett et al., 1997; Gahn & Baumiller, 2004), the calyxes of different crinoid clades (Table 5) have a tendency to disarticulate differently with the entire calyx of flexible crinoids disarticulating rapidly (hence the name of the clade), and in most disparids and cladids the arms disarticulate rapidly and the aboral cup is more robust than that of flexibles. The arms of camerates also disarticulated rapidly, but the calyx plates were

Table 5 Outline of clade-based classification of crinoids used here (from Wright, 2017a, 2017b; Wright et al. 2017; Cole, 2017, 2018)

Class Crinoidea Miller, 1821
    Subclass Camerata Wachsmuth and Springer, 1885
    Subclass Pentacrinoidea Jaekel, 1894
        Infraclass Inadunata Wachsmuth and Springer, 1885
            Parvclass Disparida Moore and Laudon, 1943
            Parvclass Cladida Moore and Laudon, 1943
                Superorder Porocrinoidea Wright, 2017a
                Superorder Flexibilia Zittel, 1895
            Magnaorder Eucldida Wright, 2017a
                Superorder Cyathoformes Wright, 2017a
                Superorder Articuliformes Wright, 2017a

typically more firmly connected and much more resistant to disarticulation. Of course, exceptions exist. For example, the basal and radial circlets of calceocrinids rapidly disarticulated along their ligament-bound synarthrial ridge, but the plates of each circlet are typically firmly connected. The Middle to Late Paleozoic Platycrinitidae and Actinocrinitidae are typically thin-walled camerates that behaved in a taphonomically similar way to typical cladids (Rhenberg et al., 2016). Further, Thompka et al. (2011) also recognized variability in genus-level disarticulation among Pennsylvanian eucladids.

Disarticulation of extinct Paleozoic echinoderm clades can be inferred based on the disarticulation behavior of extant clades. For example, edrioasteroids (Figure 6), gogiids (Figure 15), Lepidesthidae echinoids, and ophiocistioids

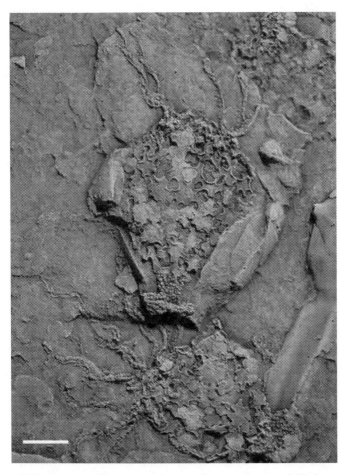

Figure 15 Latex cast with two nearly complete specimens of *Globoeocrinus globulus* from the Kaili Formation, middle Cambrian, China (see Lin et al., 2007) (photograph courtesy of J.-P Lin) (scale bar 2.5 mm).

with imbricated or very loosely connected ossicles, should have disarticulated more like asteroids and ophiuroids than like either echinoids or crinoids. Interestingly, gogiids first disarticulated in helical sheets of plates before disarticulating into individual plates (Lin et al., 2015).

The disarticulation of various blastozoan clades was potentially similar to different crinoid clades. Blastozoan brachials should have disarticulated first, followed by disarticulation of the column. Last, the theca should have disarticulated with thin-plated thecae (e.g., many "eocrinoids" and some blastoids) disarticulating more rapidly than thick-plated thecae (e.g., coronoids, and some blastoids). These inferences require verification by study of fossil occurrences with multiple echinoderm clades preserved together in various stages of disarticulation.

5 Preserving an Articulated Echinoderm

The normal progression of disarticulation must be short-circuited in order to preserve a complete echinoderm. Disarticulation of a dead animal begins rapidly, so a complete fossil must have been buried alive, and buried rapidly and permanently. After the surrounding sediment becomes lithified through cementation, an echinoderm will be preserved intact, typically yielding an ecological snapshot (Figures 1, 5–10, 13–15). Evidence of a mass mortality event not accompanied by burial left no record in the sediment (Greenstein, 1989).

Once buried, connective tissues begin to decay so if a completely preserved specimen is buried and subsequently re-exhumed prior to lithification, its skeletal elements will be disassociated and scattered along the sea floor by bedload transportation. Further, a complete, buried specimen can be disturbed by burrowing prior to lithification (Maples & Archer, 1989).

Echinoderm preservation is controlled by the interplay between burial, re-exhumation, and lithification processes. This concept is well illustrated in the Hook Head Formation of County Wexford, Ireland (Ausich & Sevastopulo, 1994). The Hook Head Formation is a Tournaisian mixed carbonate-siliciclastic ramp setting with basinal facies of the *Chonetes* beds; slope facies of the *Linoproductus*, *Michelina*, and supradolomite beds; and fair-weather wave base facies of the Bullockpark Bay Member. Echinoderm remains (principally crinoids and echinoids) are present throughout the Hook Head Formation. The facies within fair-weather wave base was dominated by frequent wave and storm activity, both transporting fossil fragments in traction along the sea floor and commonly re-exhuming previously buried fossil material. Here, the skeletal debris is completely disarticulated, and echinoderm (largely crinoidal) grainstones are common. The deepest facies of the

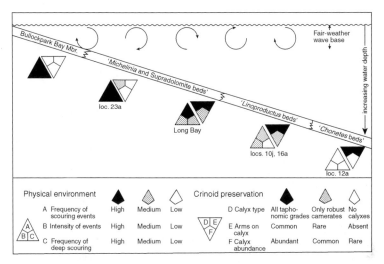

Figure 16 Interpretation of physical parameters and preservational attributes along a mixed carbonate-siliciclastic ramp in the Mississippian (Tournaisian) Hook Head Formation of County Wexford, Ireland. Note that the ideal conditions for complete crinoid crown preservation is along the mid-ramp (from Ausich & Sevastopulo, 1994, used with permission).

Chonetes beds was probably slightly above the deepest reaches of the storm-wave base. Although relatively rare, complete echinoderms are present in these beds with crinoids typically preserved with arms and short lengths of stem and rare complete echinoids. The three named units of the slope facies record a gradation in process and preservation from the fair-weather Bullockpark Bay Member to the *Chonetes* beds. Both the frequency and intensity of storm disturbance at the sea floor decreased down ramp, so frequency and thickness of storm beds decreased down slope. These physical conditions resulted in the abundance of well-preserved echinoderms peaking along the mid-ramp (Figure 16). The middle ramp setting apparently had a sufficiently high occurrence of tempestites to bury crinoids but a relatively low probability of subsequent disturbance intense enough to exhume previously buried fossils. Consequently, once buried, echinoderms had a higher probability of remaining permanently buried in the middle portions of the ramp (Ausich & Sevastopulo, 1994).

5.1 Ecological Snapshots

Rapid burial, such as by a storm, has long been recognized as a mechanism for complete echinoderm preservation (e.g., Spencer & Wright, 1966; Blake, 1967;

Sprinkle & Gutschick, 1967; Aslin, 1968; Blyth Cain, 1968; Kier, 1968; Bantz, 1969; Kesling, 1969; Lane, 1971; Rosenkrantz, 1971; Hess, 1972a; Schäfer, 1972; Lane, 1973; Brower, 1974; Blake, 1975; Brower & Veinus, 1978; Durham, 1978; Blake and Zinsmeister, 1979; Meyer et al., 1981; Smith & Paul, 1982; Sprinkle, 1982; Welch, 1984; Hess, 1985; Brett & Baird, 1986; Gale, 1986; Brett & Seilacher, 1991; Brett et al., 1991; Durham, 1993; Lane & Ausich, 1995; Taylor and Brett, 1996; Brett & Baird, 1997; Brett et al., 1997; Donovan, 1991; Ausich, 2001, 2016). The most spectacular fossil echinoderms occurrences were organisms buried alive and in situ, which have been termed "ecological snapshots" (Taylor & Brett, 1996; Ausich, 2016).

Examples of ecological snapshots are varied. They include buried hardgrounds with an attached fauna (Figure 5), such as the Brechin Lagerstätte that has a paleocommunity comprised of numerous echinoderm clades (Brett & Liddell, 1978) (Table 1) and buried shell-pavement paleocommunities with attached echinoderms (e.g., Meyer, 1990; Shroat-Lewis, McKinney et al., 2011; Shroat-Lewis, Sumrall et al., 2014; Shroat-Lewis, Greenwood et al., 2019) (Figure 6, Table 1). Ecological snapshots also include buried soft-sediment paleocommunities of both sessile and mobile echinoderms (Figures 7–10, 13–15). These examples include both rooted autochthonous individuals as well as parautochthonous sessile or mobile complete or nearly complete individuals. Numerous examples have been documented, including those mentioned in Tables 1 and 2.

6 Disarticulation and Transportation

Of all the echinoderms that inhabited the world's oceans through time, relatively few were buried and completely preserved as ecological snapshots by an obrusion deposit. Instead, a living animal was dislodged and became partially disarticulated, or disarticulated completely into discrete ossicles before burial. Echinoderm body parts passing through the digestive system of predators and scavengers were presumably another pathway to deliver disarticulated echinoderm ossicles to the sea floor (Stevenson et al., 2017). The various skeletal elements were then subject to bed load transportation across short or long distances.

Many aspects of the transportation of echinoderms and echinoderm ossicles (articulated or individual) are counterintuitive. As noted, complete echinoderm specimens typically represent a rapidly buried seafloor assemblage of autochthonous or autochthonous and parautochthonous individuals. However, transportation of complete echinoderms has been documented in many instances (e.g., Okulitch & Tovell, 1941; Seilacher, 1960, 1968; Müller, 1963; Sprinkle,

1973; Goldring & Langenstrassen, 1979; Aronson, 1987; Nebesick & Kroh, 1999). Taylor & Brett (1996) documented an unexpected occurrence of largely complete echinoderms buried within an obrusion deposit, instead of being buried on the sea floor beneath a storm bed. Thus, they had travelled some distance and could be either parautochthonous or allochthonous. Such an occurrence seems counterintuitive based on numerous reports documenting the fragile nature and rapid disarticulation of echinoderms. However, in laboratory experiments, Baumiller (2003) documented that a live crinoid could be transported a considerable distance with relatively minor disarticulation (note similar results were documented experimentally for regular echinoids (Kidwell & Baumiller, 1990)).

A second example, similar to that documented by Taylor & Brett (1996) was reported by Ausich & Meyer (1990, Figure 9) from the Fort Payne Formation of south-central Kentucky. Channels cut into the underlying Fort Payne sediments were filled with a variety of beds, including cross-bedded packstones and graded beds with a coarse basal breccia/packstone grading into finer-grained packstones and finally a siliciclastic siltstone, which was subsequently truncated by another graded unit. Crinoid crowns with some column attached are preserved within the interface between the uppermost carbonate and the siliciclastic siltstone. In at least one instance, a column along its length varied from being on the uppermost carbonate bedding surface and within the first few millimeters of the overlying siltstone. This indicates that these crinoids were transported and deposited in the waning phases of graded bedding deposition at the transition from carbonate to siltstone.

The hydrodynamic behavior of echinoderm bioclasts (complete, partial, or individual ossicles) is also unexpected because of the stereom microstructure of echinoderm skeletal elements. Using both settling behavior and entrainment thresholds of crinoid ossicles, Savarese et al. (1997) calculated that columnals of extant crinoids had an equivalent specific gravity ranging from 1.47–1.83, compared to 2.72 of solid calcite (note quartz specific gravity is 2.65). The variable shapes of crinoid ossicles adds further complications, but Savarese et al. (1997) concluded that "Columnals have settling rates and entrainment thresholds equivalent to quartz spheres with diameters less than one tenth of the diameter of the columnal (measured as the largest dimension)" (p. 141). Based on these results, one must view a bed of crinoid ossicles (Figures 2 and 4) very differently from equivalent-sized grains of solid calcite, such as those of brachiopod or mollusk shells.

Study of echinoderm alignment by currents is a topic that requires further study. If erect pelmatozoans are knocked down and immediately buried by a storm or other catastrophic event, specimens can be aligned more or less parallel in a down current direction (Figure 7). However, complete or partial specimens may not be buried immediately and became large sedimentary particles that moved along the substratum. The wide range of echinoderm morphologies suggests that different organisms will behave differently and, because of the stereom microstructure, will behave differently from an equal-sized object that is solid calcite.

Pluricolumnal orientation has been documented by Schwartzacher (1961, 1963), Nagle (1967), and Ausich and Lane (1980). Schwartzacher (1961, 1963) and Ausich and Lane (1980) documented a bimodal distribution of pluricolumnal orientations, each at an angle to the inferred current direction, whereas Nagle (1967) reported a unimodal orientation parallel to the current direction. These differences were attributed to contrasting wave and current regimes. More laboratory and field studies are required to document the range of orientations that are possible. For example, one would predict that a pluricolumnal with a crown attached would behave differently from a pluricolumnal lacking a crown.

7 Data from Disarticulation

Muscles, short ligaments, and long ligaments decay at different rates, with muscles at the most rapid rate and long ligaments the slowest. As noted, this has been documented in in situ studies and in laboratory experiments. In isocrinids, short intercolumnar ligaments connect all adjacent columnals and long, through-going ligaments bind pluricolumnal segments that include one nodal and all more distal internodals up to but not including the next most distal nodal. The proximal articulation of nodals is a synostosis articulation that is specialized for autotomy (Emson & Wilkie, 1980; Baumiller, 2003, 2008; Gorzelak 2018). Laboratory experiments on isocrinids have demonstrated that these synostoses are the planes that first separate as the column of a dead organism disarticulates (Baumiller, Llewellyn et al., 1995; Oji & Amemiya, 1998). Thus, the column first disarticulates into pluricolumnal segments of approximately equal length commonly referred to as broken sticks (Baumiller & Ausich, 1992). This pattern has also been documented in Ordovician (Ausich & Baumiller, 1998), Mississippian (Baumiller & Ausich, 1992), and Triassic (Baumiller & Hagdorn, 1995; Gorzelak, 2018) crinoids. Further, Ausich & Baumiller (1993a) applied the predicted progression of tissue decay to infer whether different Paleozoic crinoids had muscles and ligaments or only ligaments binding arm plates.

Among crinoids, specialized articulations for autotomy occur within the arms as well as the column, as noted. Autotomy is a well-documented attribute of many echinoderm clades. A skeletal segment of an echinoderm that had been autotomized would disarticulate on the sea floor in a similar fashion, based on the body part present, to a complete animal.

One of the more surprising conclusions from studying differential disarticu- lation was by Oji & Ameniya (1998). After transferring deep-sea crinoids into an aquarium, many individuals autotomized their arms and column. Columns autotomized initially into pluricolumnal segments of varying lengths with some that retained an erect posture attached to the substratum. Autotomized plurico- lumnals segments that had remained articulated for more than ~12 months were analyzed and discovered to still retain living tissue. Thus, it is possible that bedding surfaces with numerous pluricolumnals throughout the Phanerozoic included both dead and living bioclastic components (Oji & Ameniya, 1998). Regenerated columns or erect, crownless crinoid columns have also been documented in vivo (Donovan & Pawson, 1997; Veitch et al., 2015; and Sevastopulo, personal communication, 2020) as well as in fossil crinoids (Ausich & Baumiller, 1993b; Donovan & Schmidt, 2001; Lach et al., 2014).

8 Encrinites

Encrinites are carbonate rocks in which the dominate bioclasts are columnals and pluricolumnals of crinoids and other pelmatozoans. Encrinites range in size from thin, areally restricted tempestites, to flank beds on framework reefs and other carbonate buildups (Table 6, Figures 11 and 12), to regional encrinites. Regional encrinites (Ausich, 1997) are extensive carbonate deposits in which the rock is comprised of at least 50% columnals and pluricolumnals, is at least 5–10 meters thick, and has an areal extent of at least 500 km^2. The type example of a regional encrinite is the Burlington and Keokuk formations of Iowa, Missouri, and Illinois. Regional encrinite deposits occur sporadically in the stratigraphic record from the Ordovician to the Jurassic (Ausich, 1997) (Table 6). A regional encrinite sea had a coarse, poorly sorted substratum within the storm-wave base, thus the substratum was episodically mobile. This substratum would have been an unfavorable habitat for most non-pelmatozoan benthic organisms, but it was well suited for a pelmatozoan to anchor a rhizoid holdfast. Therefore, this is an example of positive taphonomic feedback (Kidwell & Jablonski, 1983) in which a disarticulating pel- matozoan provided bioclastic debris to perpetuate a substratum suitable for pelma- tozoans but unsuitable to many other benthic invertebrates. Ginsburg (2005) referred to regional encrinites as one example of a "disobedient facies."

The model for a regional encrinites is the standard interpretation of most encrinites; namely, the fossils are a transported, time-averaged amalgam of columnals and pluricolumnals from innumerable individuals that has erased

Table 6 Examples of regional encrinites; more examples are listed in Ausich (1997)

Jurassic
Smolegowia Limestone
Birkenmajer, 1977
Triassic
Lower Muschelkalk Limestone, Switzerland
Aigner, 1985
Mississippian
Burlington/ Keokuk Formations
Lane, 1978
Lane & DeKeyser, 1980
Redwall Limestone, Arizona
Gutschick et al., 1980
Kent & Rawson, 1980
Devonian
Coeymans, Keyser, and New Creek limestones, New York and West Virginia
Smosna, 1988
Edgecliff Limestone, New York
Cassa & Kissling, 1982
Silurian
Brassfield Limestone, Ohio
Ausich, 1997
Chicotte Formation, Anticosti Island, Quebec
Desrocher, 2006
James et al., 2015

any primary ecologic signal. This is true for many pelmatozoan deposits, but it should not be a universal expectation, even in extensive regional encrinites such as the Mississippian Burlington/Keokuk formations.

9 Discussion

Allochthonous echinoderm accumulations pose interesting questions about bed-load entrainment of bioclasts, but little ecological-time information about the organisms and paleocommunities can be inferred from such deposits. Also, the promise of fossil echinoderm skeletal chemistry as a guide to Ca/Mg ratios in ancient oceans (Dickson, 1995, 2001a, 2001b, 2002, 2004, 2009) has been called into question (Gorzelak, Krzykawski et al., 2016). However, autochthonous and parautochthonous echinoderm fossils are a source of varied ecological-time information.

When in the field, students should be offered the following challenge: "All benthic fossils should be interpreted as parautochthonous unless you can demonstrate they are not." Of course, benthic organisms can be preserved in their original living site (autochthonous) (Figure 5), and benthic organisms can be transported beyond the limits of their original habitat (allochthonous) by turbidites and storms. However, based on the coincident distribution of habitats, communities and lithofacies on the Grand Bahama Bank (Newell et al., 1959; Purdy, 1963, Bathurst, 1976), it is reasonable to assume an initial hypothesis that most benthic organisms were moved only a short distance from their living site and are preserved in the habitat where they lived (parautochthonous), thus providing paleocommunity information, even if time averaged.

Echinoderms are an exceptionally sensitive taphonomic tool that can be used to test between autochthonous and parautochthonous occurrences and be a means by which to determine the probability of recovery of ecological-time data that can be extracted from fossil occurrences (Baumiller, 2008). As discussed, taphonomic studies, in conjunction with in vivo and laboratory experiments, have been used to infer the distribution of various connective tissues in Paleozoic and Mesozoic crinoids. Similarly, the disarticulation sequence of fossil and extant echinoids suggests similar distributions of connective tissues and stereom interlocking of test plates through the Phanerozoic.

Connective tissue type may also be inferred in fossils using stereom microstructure, if preserved. Stereom that housed muscular tissue is distinct from that which housed ligamentary tissue (Roux, 1970, 1974a, 1974b, 1975; Macurda & Meyer, 1975; Macurda et al., 1978; Smith, 1980). Although rarely documented, stereom is preserved in some in fossil echinoderms (e.g., Lapham et al., 1976; Sevastopulo and Keegan, 1980; Dickson, 2004; Gorzelak, Krzykawski et al. 2016). If present, it may be preserved at the surface of fossil ossicles or preserved throughout the entire ossicle despite occlusion of the porosity by syntaxial cement. Although relatively rare, studies have employed stereom characteristics to understand fossil echinoderms (e.g., Lane & Macurda, 1975; Ausich, 1977, 1983; Riddle et al., 1988; Gorzelak, Gluchowski et al., 2014). As discussed, ligament arrangement present in extant isocrinids was also present in other Phanerozoic crinoids both with and without nodals or nodals with cirri (Baumiller & Ausich, 1992, 1998; Baumiller & Hagdorn, 1995; Gorzelak, 2018). Thus, the use of the ligament arrangement for autotomy in an isocrinid columnal was an exaptation of a preexisting ligament configuration.

Fossil echinoderms may be preserved in different colors. In many cases, this is undoubtedly a consequence of calcite coloration during diagenesis. However, in some instances, typically in fine-grained sediments, echinoderms are preserved with taxon-specific coloration, which preserves diagenetically stable forms of original echinoderm biomolecules (Blumer, 1951, 1960, 1962a, 1962b, 1965; Hess, 1972b; Wolkenstein, Gross et al., 2006; Wolkenstein, Gluchowski et al., 2006, 2008,; O'Malley et al., 2008, 2013, 2016) (Figures 1 and 7).

The skeleton of echinoderms, especially crinoids, is commonly closely tied to various aspects of behavior, including feeding, locomotion, etc. (e.g., Ausich, 1980; Baumiller, 2008; Baumiller, Gahn et al., 2008). Therefore, much eco-logical-time paleobiological information can be extracted from ecological snapshots of ancient sea floors. This is especially true for autochthonous, buried paleocommunities; but it is also true, with some time averaging, for both autochthonous and parautochthonous assemblages of complete specimens with or without their attachment structures. For example, the composition of a single paleocommunity can be estimated, including both biodiversity and relative abundance. Morphological variation within a species can be defined. The latter is especially true for suspension-feeding echinoderms. Arms, bra-chioles, and columns present on well-preserved specimens are directly related to niches of suspension-feeding echinoderms. A complete column indicates the position that a stalked echinoderm had within an epifaunally tiered paleocom-munity (tiering, Ausich & Bottjer, 1982; Bottjer & Ausich, 1987). Density of branching, fan area, and width of the ambulacra groove can be used to infer particle-size differentiation that further subdivides suspension-feeding niches (Lane, 1963, 1973; Ausich, 1980; Cole, 2019; Cole et al., 2019).

Although typically indirect, well-preserved burrows of infaunal echinoids can provide a means to understand infaunal tiering in post-Paleozoic paleocom-munities (e.g., Bromley & Ekdale, 1986; Kotake, 1993; Bernardi, et al., 2010). In rare instances, an echinoid may even be preserved in its burrow, which provides a definite link to its paleoecology.

Despite time-averaging effects, even encrinites can preserve ecological-time information, as noted. This is true for encrinites preserved in autochthonous facies as well as regional encrinites. Encrinites in an autochthonous facies reveal that crinoids were the dominant faunal element in that facies. Further, the occasional echinoderm crown, calyx, or theca preserved in an obtrusion deposit within the encrinite is an indication of the time-averaged species composition of that facies.

Paleoecological signals can even be retained in largely disarticulated bioclastic debris. Meyer & Meyer (1986) studied the sediment composition around a living reef and discovered that bioclasts in the sediment were a reflection of the living taxa in that habitat. Similarly, the encrinites on flank beds of crinoidal carbonate buildups in the Fort Payne Formation of south-central Kentucky are an unlikely setting to preserve ecological-time information, but they do (Meyer & Ausich,

2019). The Fort Payne Formation in south-central Kentucky is early Viséan (Mississippian) in age and was deposited at the toe-of-slope in an epicontinental basin, presumably in the lower limits of the storm-wave base (e.g., Ausich & Meyer, 1990; Greb et al., 2009). The Fort Payne Formation is a mixture of autochthonous and allochthonous facies. One example of an autochthonous crinoidal packstone buildup is the Cave Springs South buildup (Ausich & Meyer, 1990, Greb et al., 2019; Krivicich et al. 2014). This buildup has a central core with flank beds on either side dipping away from the core (Figure 17). The buildup relief today can be inferred to be a reflection of the original topographic structure on the Mississippian seafloor. The core is comprised of interbedded siliciclastic mudstone and crinoidal packstones, which contrasts with the encrinite of flanking beds. Exposures along the shores of Lake Cumberland are approximately ~15 m thick, and the diameter of this buildup is > 400 m (Figure 17). The taxonomic composition of this buildup was surveyed by dividing the outcrop into 25-m-long sectors (three along the northwestern flank of the buildup, four across the core, and three along the southeastern flank). Although crinoids and blastoids are principally preserved as an encrinite overwhelmingly dominated by columnals and pluricolumnals, a total of 563 partial crowns, thecae, partial thecae, individual plates, and columnals were identified to species or genus. A few individual plates were also diagnostic for various taxonomic levels. Most significant are radial plates. Only five radial plates are present on most crinoids, and they can commonly be identified to species if part of a well-documented fauna. The core beds were codominated by monobathrid camerate and disparid crinoids, whereas the flank beds were dominated by monobathrid camerates and was the only position where flexible crinoids and blastoids occurred (Figure 17). This symmetrical distribution of crinoids and blastoids is considered to be an indication of primary ecologic zonation across this Mississippian buildup (Meyer & Ausich, 2019)

The multi-element echinoderm skeletons can be used as a sensitive indicator to recognize ecologic-time data in a rock record that is typically dominated by time averaging (Ausich, 1980; Baumiller, 2008; Baumiller, Gahn et al., 2008). Echinoderm taphonomy can help paleontologists distinguish between: autochthonous ecological snapshots; parautochthonous ecological snapshots; parautochthonous, time-averaged assemblages that retain some ecological-time signals; completely time-averaged parautochthonous assemblages; and time-averaged allochthonous assemblages. The principle amount of taphonomic study on echinoderms has been completed on crinoids and echinoids. Much more work is required to better understand ecological-time in other clades. Echinoderm taphonomy and that of other clades can be used to extract time-related taphonomic data and are a powerful tool to better understand the history of life on Earth.

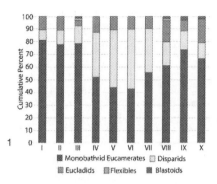

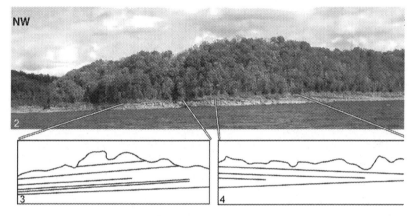

Figure 17 Distribution of crinoids and blastoids across the Cave Springs South crinoidal packstone buildup; Fort Payne Formation, Mississippian (early Viséan) south-central Kentucky (from Meyer and Ausich, 2019, used with permission). **(1)** Histogram indicating the percent of each pelmatozoan clade in each sector across the buildup. **(2)** Photograph of shoreline exposure of the Cave Springs South buildup. **(3)** Depiction of the flank beds on the northwestern side of the buildup. **(4)** Depiction of the flank beds on the southeastern side of the buildup.

Repositories and Institutional Abbreviations

Illustrated specimens are housed in the following museums: BC, Beloit College; CMCIP, Cincinnati Museum Center, Cincinnati, Ohio; Field Museum of Natural History, Chicago, Illinois; OSU, Orton Geological Museum, Ohio State University; RM, Swedish Museum of Natural History, Stockholm; TMM, Texas Memorial Museum, University of Texas; UMMP, University of Michigan Museum of Paleontology.

References

Adkins, W. S. (1928). Handbook of Texas Cretaceous fossils. *University of Texas Bulletin*, **2838**

Aigner, T. (1985). *Storm depositional systems: Dynamic stratigraphy in modern and ancient shallow-marine sequences*. Lecture Notes in the Earth Sciences, 3, New York, Springer-Verlag.

Allison, P. A. (1990). Variation in rates of decay and disarticulation of Echinodermata: Implications for the application of actualistic data. *PALAIOS*, **5**, 432–440.

Aronson, R. B. (1987). Predation on fossil and Recent ophiuroids. *Paleobiology*, **13**, 187–192.

Aronson, R. B., & Blake, D. B. (1997). Evolutionary paleoecology of dense ophiuroids populations. In J. A. Waters & C. G. Maples, eds., *Geobiology of Echinoderm. Paleontological Society Papers*, **3**, pp. 107–119.

Aslin, C. J. (1968). Echinoid preservation in Upper Estuarine Limestone of Blisworth Northamptonshire. *Geological Magazine*, **105**, 506–518.

Ausich, W. I. (1977). The functional morphology and evolution of *Pisocrinus* (Crinoidea: Silurian). *Journal of Paleontology*, **51**, 672–686.

Ausich, W. I. (1980). A model for niche differentiation in Lower Mississippian crinoid communities. *Journal of Paleontology*, **54**, 273–288.

Ausich, W. I. (1983). Functional morphology and feeding dynamics of the Early Mississippian crinoid *Barycrinus asteriscus*. *Journal of Paleontology*, **57**, 31–41.

Ausich, W. I. (1997). Regional encrinites: A vanished lithofacies. In C. E. Brett and G. C. Baird, eds., *Paleontological Events: Stratigraphic, Ecologic and Evolutionary Implications*. New York: Columbia University Press, pp. 509–519.

Ausich, W. I. (2001). Echinoderm taphonomy. In J. Lawrence and M. Jangoux, eds., *Echinoderm Studies*, Vol. 6. Rotterdam: A. A. Balkema Press, pp. 171–227.

Ausich, W. I. (2016). Fossil species as data: A perspective from echinoderms. In W. D. Allmon & M. M. Yacobucci, eds., *Species and Speciation in the Fossil Record*. Chicago, IL: University of Chicago Press, pp. 301–311.

Ausich, W. I. , & Baumiller, T. K. (1993a). Taphonomic method for determining muscular articulations in fossil crinoids. *PALAIOS*, **8**, 477–484.

Ausich, W. I., & Baumiller, T. K. (1993b). Column regeneration in an Ordovician crinoid (Echinodermata): Paleobiologic implications. *Journal of Paleontology*, **67**, 1068–1070.

Ausich, W. I. , & Baumiller, T. K. (1998). Disarticulation patterns in Ordovician crinoids: Implications for the evolutionary history of connective tissue in the Crinoidea. *Lethaia*, **31**: 113–123.

Ausich, W. I. , & Bottjer, D. J. (1982). Tiering in suspension-feeding communities on soft substrata throughout the Phanerozoic. *Science*, **216**, 173–174.

Ausich, W. I. , & Lane, N. G. (1980). Platform communities and rocks of the Borden Siltstone Delta (Mississippian) along the south shore of Monroe Reservoir, Monroe County, Indiana. In R. H. Shaver, ed., *Field Trips 1980 from the Indiana University Campus*, Bloomington: Indiana University, pp. 36–67.

Ausich, W. I. , & Meyer, D. L. (1990). Origin and composition of carbonate buildups and associated facies in the Fort Payne Formation (Lower Mississippian, south-central Kentucky): An integrated sedimentologic and paleoecologic analysis. *Geological Society of America Bulletin*, **102**, 129–146.

Ausich, W. I. , & Sevastopulo, G. D. (1994). Taphonomy of Lower Carboniferous crinoids from the Hook Head Formation, Ireland. *Lethaia*, **27**, 245–256.

Balaústegui, Z, Muñiz, F., Nebelsick, J. H., Domènech, R., & Martinell, J. (2012). Echinoderm ichnology: Bioturbation, bioerosion and related processes. *Journal of Paleontology*, **91**, 643–661.

Bantz, H. –U. (1969). Echinoidea uns Plattenkalken der Altmühlabhre Biostratyinomie. *Erlanger Geologische Abhandlunge*, **78**, 1–35.

Bathurst, R. G. C. (1976). *Carbonate Sediments and Their Diagensis*, 2nd ed. Amsterdam: Elsevier.

Baumiller, T. K. (2003). Experimental and biostratinomic disarticulation of crinoids: Taphonomic implications In Echinoderm Research 2001. In J.-P. Féral & B. David, eds., *Paleontological Events: Stratigraphic, Ecologic, and Evolutionary Implications*. Lisse: Swets and Zietlinger, pp. 243–248.

Baumiller, T. K. (2008). Crinoid ecological morphology. *Annual Reviews in the Earth Sciences*, **36**, 221–249.

Baumiller, T. K., & Ausich, W. I. (1992). The "broken stick" model as a null hypothesis for crinoid stalk taphonomy and as a guide to the distribution of connective tissues in fossils. *Paleobiology*, **18**, 288–298.

Baumiller, T. K. , & Hagdorn, H. (1995). Taphonomy as a guide to functional morphology of *Holocrinus*, the first post-Paleozoic crinoid. *Lethaia*, **28**, 221–228.

Baumiller, T. K., Gahn, F. J., Hess, H. , & Messing, C. G. (2008). Taphonomy as an indicator of behavior among fossil crinoid. In W. I. Ausich & G. D. Webster, eds., *Echinoderm Paleobiology*, Bloomington: Indiana University Press, pp. 7–20.

Baumiller, T. K., Llewellyn, G., Messing, C. G., & Ausich, W. I. (1995). Taphonomy and autotomy of isocrinid stalks: Influence of decay and autotomy. *Palaios*, **10**, 87–95.

Bell, B. M. (1976). A study of North American Edrioasteroidea. *New York State Museum Memoir*, **21**, 447 p.

Bernardi, M., Boschele, S., Ferretti, P., & Avanzini, M. (2010). Echinoid burrow *Bichordites monastiriensis* from the Oligocene of NE Italy. *Acta Palaeontologica Polonica*, **55**, 479–486.

Birkenmajer, K. (1977). Jurassic and Cretaceous lithostratigraphic unites of the Leinny Klippen Belt, Carpathians, Poland. *Studia Geologica Polonica*, **45**, 1–158.

Blake, D. B. (1967). Pre-burial abrasion of articulated asteroid skeletons. *Paleobios*, **2**, 4 p.

Blake, D. B. (1975). A new west American Miocene species of the modern Australian ophiuroids. *Ophiocrassota. Journal of Paleontology*, **49**, 501–506.

Blake, D. B., & Zinsmeister, W. J. (1979). Two early Cenozoic sea stars (Class Asteroidea) from Seymour Island, Antarctica Peninsula. *Journal of Paleontology*, 53, 1145–1154.

Blake, D. B., Guensburg, T. E., Sprinkle, J. , & Sumrall, C. D. (2007). A new phylogenetically significant Early Ordovician asteroid (Echinodermata). *Journal of Paleontology*, **81**, 1100–1101.

Blumer, M. (1951). Fossile Kohlenwassertoffe und Farbstoffe in Kalketeinen. *Mikrochemie*, **36/37**, 1048–1055

Blumer, M. (1960). Pigments of a fossil echinoderm. *Nature*, **188**, 1100–1101.

Blumer, M. (1962a). The organic chemistry of a fossil – I: The structure of fringelite-pigments. *Geochimica et Cosmochimica Acta*, **26**, 225–227.

Blumer, M. (1962b). The organic chemistry of a fossil – II: Some rare poly-nuclear hydrocarbons. *Geochimica et Cosmochimica Acta*, **26**, 228–230.

Blumer, M. (1965). Organic pigments: Their long-term fate. *Science*, **149**, 722–726.

Blyth Cain, J. D. (1968). Aspects of the depositional environment and paleoecology of crinoidal limestones. *Scottish Journal of Geology*, **4**, 191–208.

Bottjer, D. J. , & W. I. Ausich. (1987). Phanerozoic development of tiering in soft substrata suspension-feeding communities. *Paleobiology* **12**, 400–420.

Breton, G. (1997). Deux étoiles de mer du Bajocien du nord-est du basin de Paris (France): leur allies actuels sond des fossils vivants. *Bulletin trimestriel de la Société Géologique de Normandie et des Amis du Museum du Havre*, **84**, 23–34.

Brett, C. E. (1985). Pelmatozoan echinoderms on Silurian bioherms in western New York and Ontario. *Journal of Paleontology*, **59**, 820–838.

Brett, C. E. (1995). Sequence stratigraphy, biostratigraphy, and taphonomy in shallow marine environments. *PALAIOS*, **10**, 597–616.

Brett, C. E., & Baird, G. (1986). Comparative taphonomy: A key to paleoenvironmental interpretation based on fossil preservation. *PALAIOS*, **1**, 207–227.

Brett, C. E., & Baird, G. (1997). Epiboles, outages, and ecological evolutionary bioevents: Taphonomy, ecological, and biogeographic factors. In C. E. Brett & G. Baird, eds., *Paleontological Events: Stratigraphic, Ecologic, and Evolutionary Implications*. New York: Columbia University Press, pp. 249–284.

Brett, C. E., & Liddell, W. D. (1978). Preservation and paleoecology of a Middle Ordovician hardground community. *Paleobiology*, **4**, 329–348.

Brett, C. E., & Seilacher, A. (1991). Fossil-Lagerstätten: a taphonomic consequence of event sedimentation. In G. Einsele, W. Ricken & A. Seilacher, eds., *Cycles and Events in Stratigraphy*. New York, Berlin: Springer Verlag, pp. 283–297.

Brett, C. E., & Taylor, W. L. (1997). The *Homocrinus* beds: Silurian Lagerstätten of western New York and southern Ontario. In C. E. Brett & G. Baird, eds., *Paleontological Events: Stratigraphic, Ecologic, and Evolutionary Implications*. New York: Columbia University Press, pp. 181–499.

Brett, C. E., Deline, B. L., & McLaughlin, P. I. (2008). Attachment, facies distribution, and life history strategies in crinoids from the Upper Ordovician of Kentucky. In W. I. Ausich & G. D. Webster, eds., *Echinoderm Paleobiology*. Bloomington: Indiana University Press, pp. 23–52.

Brett, C. E., Dick, V. E., & Baird, G. C. (1991). Comparative taphonomy and paleoecology of Middle Devonian dark gray and black shale facies from Western New York. In E. Landing & C. E. Brett, eds., Dynamic Stratigraphy and Depositional Environments of the Hamilton Group (Middle Devonian) in New York State, Part II. *New York State Museum Bulletin*, **469**, pp. 5–36.

Brett, C. E., Moffat, H. A., & Taylor, W. L. (1997). Echinoderm taphonomy, taphofacies, and Lagerstätten. In J. A. Waters & C. G. Maples, eds., *Geobiology of Echinoderms. Paleontological Society Papers*, 3, p147–190.

Bridges, P. H., Gutteridge, P., & Pickard, N. A. H. (1995). The environmental setting of Early Carboniferous mud-mounds. In C. L. V. Monty, D. W. J. Bosence, P. H. Bridges & B. R. Pratt, eds., *Carbonate Mud-mounds Their Origin and Evolution*. Oxford: Blackwell Science, pp. 171–190.

Bromley, R. G., & Ekdale, A. A. (1986). Composite ichnofabrics and tiering of burrows. *Geological Magazine*, **123**, 59–65.

Brower, J. C. (1974). Crinoids from the Girardeau Limestone (Ordovician). *Palaeontographica Americana*, **7**, 259–499.

Brower, J. C., & Veinus, J. (1978). Middle Ordovician crinoids from the Twin Cities area of Minnesota. *Bulletins of American Paleontology*, **74**, 369–506.

Carozzi, A. V., & Soderman, J. G. (1962). Petrography of Mississippian (Borden) crinoidal limestones at Stobo, Indiana. *Journal of Sedimentary Petrology*, **32**, 397–414.

Cassa, M. R., & Kissling, D. L. (1982). Carbonate facies of the Onondaga and Boise Blanc Formations Niagara Peninsula, Ontario. In E. J. Buehler & P. E. Calkin, eds., *Guidebook for Field Trips in Western New York, Northern Pennsylvania, and Adjacent Southern Ontario.* New York State Geological Association 54th Annual Meeting, 55–97. Rocky Mountain Paleogeography Symposium I, Paleozoic Paleogeography of the West-Central United States, pp. 111–128.

Cole, S. R. (2017). Phylogeny and morphologic evolution of the Ordovician Camerata (Class Crinoidea, Phylum Echinodermata). *Journal of Paleontology*, **91**, 815–828.

Cole, S. R. (2018). Phylogeny and evolutionary history of diplobathrid crinoids (Echinodermata). *Palaeontology*, **62**, 357–373.

Cole, S. R. (2019). Hierarchical controls on extinction selectivity across the diplobathrid crinoid phylogeny. *Paleobiology*, doi: https://doi.org/10.1017/pab.2019.37.

Cole, S. R., Wright, D. W., & Ausich, W. I. (2019). Phylogenetic community paleoecology of one of the earliest complex crinoid faunas (Brechin Lagerstätte, Ordovician). *Palaeogeography, Palaeoclimatology, Palaeoecology*, **521**, 82–98.

Cornell, S. R., Brett, C. E., & Sumrall, C. D. (2003). Paleoecology and taphonomy of an edrioasteroid-dominated hardground association from tentaculitid limestones in the Early Devonian of New York: A Paleozoic rocky peritidal community. *PALAIOS*, **18**, 212–224.

Desrocher, A. (2006). Rocky shoreline deposits in the Lower Silurian (upper Llandovery, Telychian) Chicotte Formation, Anticosti Island, Quebec. *Canadian Journal of Earth Sciences*, **43**, 1205–1214.

Dickson, J. A. D. (1995). Paleozoic Mg calcite preserved: Implications for the Carboniferous ocean. *Geology*, **23**, 535–538.

Dickson, J. A. D. (2001a). Diagenesis and crystal caskets: Echinoderm Mg calcite transformation. Dry Canyon, New Mexico, U.S.A. *Journal of Sedimentary Research*, **71**, 764–777.

Dickson, J. A. D. (2001b). Transformation of echinoid Mg calcite skeletons by heating. *Geochimica, Geocosmochimica, Acta*, **65**, 443–454.

Dickson, J. A. D. (2002). Fossil echinoderms as monitor of the Mg/Ca ratio of Phanerozoic oceans. *Science*, **298**, 1222–1224.

Dickson, J. A. D. (2004). Echinoderm skeletal preservation: Calcite-aragonite seas and the Mg/Ca ratio of Phanerozoic oceans. *Journal of Sedimentary Research*, **74**, 355–365.

Dickson, J. A. D. (2009). Mississippian paleocean chemistry from biotic and abiotic carbonate, Muleshoe Mound, Lake Valley Formation, New Mexico, U.S.A. – discussion. *Journal of Sedimentary Research*, **79**, 40–41.

Donovan, S. K. (1991). Taphonomy of echinoderms: Calcareous multi-element skeletons in the marine environment. In S. K. Donovan, ed., *The Process of Fossilization*. London: Belhaven, pp. 241–269.

Donovan, S. K., & Pawson, D. L. (1997). Proximal growth of the column in bathycrinid crinoids (Echinodermata) following decapitation. *Bulletin of Marine Science*, **61**, 571–579.

Donovan, S. K., & Schmidt, D. A. (2001). Survival of crinoid stems following decapitation: Evidence from the Ordovician and palaeobiological implications. *Lethaia*, **34**, 263–370.

Durham, J. W. (1978). Polymorphism in the Pliocene sand dollar *Merriamaster* (Echinodermata). *Journal of Paleontology*, **52**, 275–286.

Durham, J. W. (1993). Observations on the Early Cambrian helicoplacoid echinoderms. *Journal of Paleontology*, **67**, 590–604.

Emson, R. H., & Wilkie, I. C. (1980). Fission and autotomy in echinoderms. *Oceanography and Marine Biology*, **18**, 155–250.

Franzén, C. (1982). A Silurian crinoid thanatotope from Gotland. *Geologiska Föreningens i Stockholm Förhandlingar*, **103**, 469–490.

Ginsburg, R. N. (2005). Disobedient sediments can feedback on their transportation, deposition, and geomorphology. Sedimentary Geology, **175**, 9–18.

Gahn, F. J., & Baumiller, T. K. (2004). A bootstrap analysis for comparative taphonomy as applied to Early Mississippian (Kinderhookian) crinoids from the Wassonville cycle of Iowa. *PALAIOS*, **19**, 17–38.

Gale, A. S. (1986). Goniasteridae (Asteroidea, Echinodermata) from the Late Cretaceous of north-west Europe. I. Introduction. The genera Metopaster and Recurvaster. *Mesozoic Research*, **1**, 1–69.

Glass, A. (2005). Two isorophid edrioasteroids (Echinodermata) encrusting conularids from the Hunsrück Slate (Lower Devonian, Emsian; Rheinisches Schiefergebirge) of Germany. *Senckenbergiana lethaea*, **85**, 31–37.

Glynn, P. W. (1984). An amphionid worm predator of the crown-of-thorns sea star and general predation on asteroids in eastern and western Pacific coral reefs. *Bulletin of Marine Science*, **35**, 54–71.

Goldring, R., & Laggenstrassen, F. (1979). Open shelf and near-shore clastic facies in the Devonian. *Special Papers in Palaeontology*, **23**, 81–97.

Goldring, B., & Stephenson, D. G. (1972). The depositional environment of three starfish beds. Neues Jahrbuch für Geologie und Paläontologie – Abhandlungen, **10**, 611–624.

Gorzelak, P. (2018). Microstructural evidence for stalk autotomy in *Holocrinus*: The oldest stem-group isocrinid. *Palaeogeography, Palaeoclimatology, Palaeoecology*, **506**, 202–207. DOI: doi.org/10.1016/j.palaeo.2018.06.036.

Gorzelak, P., Głuchowski, E., & Salamon, M. (2014). Reassessing the improbability of a muscular crinoid stem. *Scientific Reports*, **4**. DOI: 10:1038/srep06049.

Gorzelak, P., Krzykawski, T., & Stolarski, J. (2016). Diagenesis of echinoderm skeletons: Constraints on paleoseawater Mg/Ca reconstructions. *Global and Planetary Change*, **144**, 142–157.

Gorzelak, P., Stolarski, J., Mazur, M., & Meibom, A. (2012). Micro- to nano-structure and geochemistry of extant crinoidal echinoderm skeletons. *Geobiology*. DOI: 10:1111/gbi.12012.

Greb, S. F., Potter, P. E., Meyer, D. L., & Ausich, W. I. (2009). Mud Mounds, Paleoslumps, Crinoids, and More; The Geology of the Fort Payne Formation at Lake Cumberland, South-central Kentucky. *Kentucky Geological Survey Guidebook*. www.professionalgeologist.org/guidebook.thtm; last accessed March 27, 2019.

Greenstein, B. J. (1989). Mass mortality of the West-Indian echinoid *Diadema antillarum* (Echinodermata: Echinoidea): A natural experiment in taphonomy. *PALAIOS*, **4**, 487–492.

Greenstein, B. J. (1990). Taphonomic biasing of subfossil echinoid populations adjacent to St. Croix, U.S.V.I. In D. K. Larve, ed., *Transactions of the 12th International Caribbean Congress, Miami Geological Society*, pp. 290–300.

Greenstein, B. J. (1991). An integrated study of echinoid taphonomy: Predictions for the fossil record of four echinoid families. *PALAIOS*, **6**, 519–540.

Greenstein, B. J. (1992). Taphonomic bias and the evolutionary history of the family Cidaridae (Echinodermata: Echinoidea). *Paleobiology*, **18**, 50–79.

Grun, T. B., Mancosu, A., Bealaústegui, Z., & Nebelsick, J. H. (2018). The taphonomy of *Clypeaster*: A paleontological tool to identify stable structures in natural shell systems. Neues Jahrbuch für Geologie und Paläontologie – Abhandlungen, **289**, 189–202. DOI:10.1127/njgpa/2018/0737.

Guensburg, T. E. (1988). Systematics, functional morphology, and life modes of late Ordovician edrioasteroids, Orchard Creek Shale, southern Illinois. *Journal of Paleontology*, **62**, 110–126.

Guensburg, T. E., & Sprinkle, J. (1994). Revised phylogeny and functional interpretation of the Edrioasteroidea based on new taxa from the Early Ordovician of eastern Utah. *Fieldiana (Geology)*, **29**, 43 p.

Guensburg, T. E., & Sprinkle, J. (1995). Origin of echinoderms in the Paleozoic evolutionary fauna: The role of substrates. *PALAIOS*, **10**, 437–453.

Gutschick, R. C., Sandberg, C. A., & Sando, W. J. (1980). Mississippian shelf margin and carbonate platform from Montana to Nevada. In T. D. Fouch & E. R. Magathan, eds., *Rocky Mountain Paleogeography Symposium I, Paleozoic Paleogeography of the West-Central United States*, pp. 111–128.

Hagdorn, H., & Schulz, M. (1996). Echinodermen-Konservatlagerstätten im Unteren Muschelkalk Osthessens, 1. Die Bimbacher Seelilienbank von Grossenlüder-Bimbach. Geologisches Jahrbuch Hessen, **124**, 97–122.

Hagdorn, H., Berra, F., & Tintori, A. (2018). *Encrinus aculeatus* von Meyer, 1849 (Crinoidea, Echinodermata) from the Middle Triassic of Bal Brembana (Alpi Orobie, Bergamo, Italy). *Swiss Journal of Paleontology*, **137**, 211–224. DOI: doi.org/10.1007/s13358-018-1270-0.

Hess, H. (1972a). *Chariocrinus* n. gen. für *Isocrinus andraea* Desor aus dem unteren Hauptrogenstein (Bajocien) des Basler Juras. *Eclogae Geologicae Helvetiae*, **65**, 197–210.

Hess, H. (1972b). The fringilites of the Jurassic Sea. *CIBA-GEIGY Journal*, **2**, 14–17.

Hess, H. (1985). Schlangensterne und Seelilien aus dem unteren Lias von Hallau (Kanton Schaffhausen). *Sonderdruck aus den Mitteilungen der Naturforschenden Gesellschoft Schaffhausen*, **33**, 1–15.

Jackson, W. D., & De Keyser, T. (1984). Microfacies analysis of Muleshoe Mound (Early Mississippian), Sacramento Mountains, New Mexico: A point-source depositional model Part II. West Texas Geological Society Bulletin, **23** (6), 6–10.

Jaekel, O. (1894). Über die Morphogenie und Phylogenic der Crinoiden. *Sitzungsberichten der Gesellschaft Naturforschender Freunde, Jargang 1894*, **4**, 101–121.

Jagt, J. W. M., Thuy, B., Donovan, S. K., et al. (2014). A starfish bed in the middle Miocene Grand Bay Formation of Carriacou, The Grenadines (West Indies). *Geological Magazine*, **151**, 381–393.

James, N. P., Desrochers A., & Kyser, T. K. (2015). Polygenetic (polyphase) karsted hardground omission surfaces in lower Silurian neritic limestones: Anticosti Island, eastern Canada. *Journal of Sedimentary Research*, **85**, 1138–1154.

Kammer, T. W., Tissue, E. C., & Wilson, M. A. (1987). *Neoisorophusella*, a new edrioasteroid genus from the Upper Mississippian of the Eastern United States. *Journal of Paleontology*, **61**, 1033–1042.

Kent, W. N., & Rawson, R. R. (1980). Depositional environments of the Mississippian Redwall Limestone in northeastern Arizona. In T. D. Fouch & E. R. Magathan, eds., *Rocky Mountain Paleogeography Symposium I, Paleozoic Paleogeography of the West-Central United States*, pp. 101–109.

Kesling, R. V. (1969). A new brittle-star from the Middle Devonian Arkona Shale of Ontario. *University of Michigan Museum of Paleontology Contributions*, **23**, 37–51.

Kesling, R. V., & Le Vasseur, D. (1971). *Strataster ohioensis*, a new Early Mississippian brittle-star, and the paleoecology of its community. *Contributions to the Museum of Paleontology, University of Michigan*, **23**, 305–341.

Kidwell, S. M., & Baumiller, T. K. (1990). Experimental disintegration of regular echinoids: Roles of temperature, oxygen, and decay thresholds. *Paleobiology*, **16**, 247–271.

Kidwell, S. M., & Jablonski, D. (1983). Taphonomic feedback: Ecological consequences of shell accumulation. In M. J. S. Tevesz & P. L. McCall, eds., *Biotic Interactions in Recent and Fossil Communities*. New York: Plenum Press, pp. 195–248.

Kidwell, S. M., Fürsich, & T. Aigner. (1986). Conceptual framework for the analysis and classification of fossil concentrations. *PALAIOS*, **1**, 228–238.

Kier, P. M. (1968). Triassic echinoids from the North America. *Journal of Paleontology*, **42**, 1000–1006

Kier, P. M. (1977). The poor fossil record of the regular echinoid. *Paleobiology*, **3**, 168–174.

Koch, D. L., & Strimple, H. L. (1968). A new upper Devonian cystoid attached to a discontinuity surface. *Iowa Geological Survey Report of Investigations*, **5**, 49 p.

Kotake, N. (1993). Tiering of trace fossil assemblages in Plio-Pleistocene bathyal deposits of Boso Peninsula, Japan. *PALAIOS*, **8**, 544–553.

Krivicich, E. B., Ausich, W. I., & Meyer, D. L. (2014). Crinoid assemblages from the Fort Payne Formation (late Osagean, early Viséan, Mississippian) from Kentucky, Tennessee, and Alabama. *Journal of Paleontology*, **88**, 1154–1162.

Kroh, A., & Nebelsick, J. H. (2003). Echinoid assemblages as a tool for palaeoenvironmental reconstruction – An example from the early Miocene of Egypt. *Palaeogeography, Palaeoclimatology, Palaeoecology*, **201**, 157–177.

Kühl, G., Bartels, C., Briggs, D. E. G., & Rust, J. (2012). *Visions of a Vanished World*. New Haven: Yale University Press, 128 p.

Lane, H. R. (1978). The Burlington Shelf (Mississippian, north-central North America). *Geologica et Paleontologica*, **12**, 165–176.

Lane, H. R., & DeKeyser, T. L. (1980). Paleogeography of the late Early Mississippian (Tournaisian 3) in the central and southwestern United States. In T. D. Fouch and Magathan, E., eds., *Paleozoic paleogeography of west-central United States: West-central United States*. West-Central United States Paleogeographic Symposium, **1**, pp. 149–162.

Lane, N. G. (1963). The Berkeley crinoid collection from Crawsfordsville, Indiana. *Journal of Paleontology*, **3**, 1001–1008.

Lane, N. G. (1971). Crinoids and reefs. *Proceedings of the First North American Paleontological convention*, **1**, 1430–1443.

Lane, N. G. (1973). Paleontology and paleoecology of the Crawfordsville fossil site (Upper Osagian. Indiana). *California University Publications in the Geological Sciences*, **99**, 141 p.

Lane, N. G., & Ausich, W. I. (1995). Interreef crinoid faunas from the Mississinewa Shale Member of the Wabash Formation (northern Indiana: Silurian; Echinodermata). *Journal of Paleontology*, **69**, 1090–1106.

Lane, N. G., & Macurda, D. B., Jr. (1975). New evidence for muscular articulations in Paleozoic crinoids. *Paleobiology*, **1**, 59–62.

Lapham, K. E., Ausich, W. I., & Lane, N. G. (1976). A technique for developing the stereom of fossil crinoid ossicles. *Journal of Paleontology*, **50**, 245–248.

Latch, R., Trzęsoik, D., & Szopa. P. (2014). Life and death: an intriguing history of a Jurassic crinoid. *Paleontological Journal*, **18**, 40–44.

Laudon L. R., & Beane, B. H. (1937). The crinoid fauna of the Hampton Formation at LeGrand, Iowa. *University of Iowa Studies*, **17**, 227–272.

Le Clare, E. E. (1993). Effects of anatomy and environment on the relative preservation of asteroids: a biomechanical observation. *PALAIOS*, **8**, 233–243.

Lees, A., & Miller, J. (1995). Waulsortian banks. In C. L. V. Monty, D. W. J. Bosence, P. H.Bridges, & B. R. Pratt, eds. *Carbonate Mudmounds Their Origin and Evolution* Oxford: Blackwell Science, pp. 191–271.

Lewis, R. (1980). Taphonomy. In T. W. Broadhead and J. A. Waters, eds., *Echinoderms: Notes for a Short Course*. Knoxville: University of Tennessee Department of Geological Sciences Studies in Geology, pp. 40–58.

Lewis, R. (1986). Relative rates of skeletal disarticulation in modern ophiuroids and Paleozoic crinoids. Geological Society of America Abstracts with Programs, **18**, 672.

Liddell, W. D. (1975). Recent crinoid biostratinomy. Geological *Society of America, Abstracts with Programs*, **7**, 1169.

Lin, J.-P., Ausich, W. I., & Zhao, Y.-L. (2008). Settling strategy of stalked echinoderms from the Kaili Biota (middle Cambrian), Guizhou Province, China. *Palaeogeography, Palaeoclimatology, Palaeoecology*, **258**, 213–221.

Lin, J.-P., Ausich, W. I., Zhao, Y.-L., & Peng, J. (2007). Taphonomy, palaeo-cological implications, and colouration of Cambrian gogiid echinoderms from Guizhou Province, China. *Geological Magazine*, **145**, 17–36. doi:10.1017/S0016756807003901 (published on paper in 2008 volume)

Lin, J.-P., Ausich, W. I., Zhao, Y.-L., Peng, J., & T. S. Tai (2015). Crypto-helical body plan in partially disarticulated gogiids from the Cambrian of South China. *Palaeoworld*, **24**, 393–399.

Lowenstam, H. A. (1957). Niagaran reefs in the Great Lakes region. *Geological Society of America Memoir*, **67**, 215–248.

MacQueen, R. W., Ghent, E. D., & Davies, G. R. (1974). Magnesium distribution in living and fossil specimens of the echinoid *Peronella lesueuia* Agassiz, Shark Bay, Western Australia. *Journal of Sedimentary Petrology*, **44**, 60–69.

Macurda, D. B., Jr., & Meyer, D. L. (1975). The microstructure of the crinoid endoskeleton. *University of Kansas Paleontological Institute Paper*, **74**, 22 p.

Macurda, D. B., Jr., Meyer, D. L., & Roux, M. (1978). The crinoid stereom. In R. C. Moore & C. Teichert, eds., *Treatise on Invertebrate Paleontology, Part T., Echinodermata 2, 1.* Lawrence, KS, and Boulder, CO: University of Kansas Press and Geological Society of America, pp. 217–232.

Mancousa, A., & Nebelsick, J. H. (2013). Multiple routes to mass accumulations of clypeasteroid echinoids: a comparative analysis of Miocene echinoids beds of Sardinia. *Palaeogeography, Palaeoclimatology, Palaeoecology*, **374**, 173–186.

Mancousa, A., & Nebelsick, J. H. (2015). The origin and paleoecology of clypeasteroid assemblages from different shelf settings of the Miocene of Sardinia, Italy. *PALAIOS*, **30**, 273–287.

Mancousa, A., & Nebelsick, J. H. (2017). Ecomorphological and taphonomic gradients in clypeasteroid-dominated echinoderm assemblages along a mixed siliciclastic-carbonate shelf from the early Miocene of northern Sardinia, Italy. *Acta Palaeontologica Polonica*, **62**, 627–646.

Maples, C. G., & Archer, A. W. (1989). Paleoecological and sedimentological significance of bioturbated crinoid calyces. *PALAIOS*, **4**, 379–383.

Meyer, D. L. (1971). Post-mortem disarticulation of Recent crinoids and ophiuroids under natural conditions. *Geological Society of America, Abstracts with Programs*, **3**, 645.

Meyer, D. L. (1990). Population paleoecology and comparative taphonomy of two edrioasteroid (Echinodermata) pavements: Upper Ordovician of Kentucky and Ohio. *Historical Biology*, **4**, 155–178.

Meyer, D. L., & Ausich, W. I. (2019). Ecological and taphonomic fidelity in fossil crinoid accumulations. *PALAIOS*, **34**, 575–583. DOI: http://dx.doi.org /10.2110/palo.2019.032.

Meyer, D. L., & Meyer, K. B. (1986). Biostratinomy of Recent crinoids (Echinodermata) at Lizard Island, Great Barrier Reef, Australia. *PALAIOS*, **1**, 294–301.

Meyer, D. L., & Weaver, T. R. (1980). Biostratinomy of crinoid-dominated communities in the lower Bull Fork Formation (Upper Ordovician) of southwestern Ohio. *Geological Society of America Abstracts with Programs*, **12**, 251.

Meyer, D. L., Ausich, W. I., Bohl, D. T., Norris, W. A., & Potter, P. E. (1995). Carbonate mud-mounds in the Fort Payne Formation (lower Carboniferous) Cumberland Saddle region, Kentucky and Tennessee USA. In C. L. V. Monty, D. W. J. Bosence, P. H.Bridges, & B. R. Pratt, eds., *Carbonate Mudmounds Their Origin and Evolution* Oxford: Blackwell Science, pp. 273–287.

Meyer, D. L., Ausich, W. I., & Terry, R. E. (1990). Comparative taphonomy of echinoderms in carbonate facies: Fort Payne Formation (Lower Mississippian) of Kentucky and Tennessee. *PALAIOS*, **4**, 533–552. (this 1989 issue not published until 1990).

Meyer, D. L., Tobin, R. C., Pryor, W. A., et al. (eds.) (1981). Stratigraphy, sedimentology, and paleoecology of the Cincinnatian Series (Upper Ordovician) in the vicinity of Cincinnati, Ohio. In T. G.Roberts, (ed.), *Geological Society of America Cincinnati 1981, Field Trip Guidebooks*, Falls Church, VA: American Geological Institute pp. 31–72.

Milam, M. J., Meyer, D. L., Dattilo, B. J., & Hunda, B. R. (2017). Taphonomy of an Ordovician crinoid Lagerstätte from Kentucky. *Palaios*, 32: 166–180, figs. 1–15.

Miller, J. S. (1821). *A natural history of the Crinoidea, or lily-shaped animals; with observations on the genera, Asteria, Euryale, Comatula and Marsupites*. Bristol, UK: Bryan and Co.

Moore, R. C., & Laudon, L. R. (1943). Evolution and classification of Paleozoic crinoids. *Geological Society of America Special Paper*, **46**, 151 p.

Moran, P. J. (1992). Preliminary observations of the decomposition of crown-of-thorns starfish, *Acanthaster planci* (L.). *Coral Reefs*, **11**, 115–118.

Müller, A. H. (1963). *Lehrbuch der Paläozoologie I. Allgemeine Grudlagen, Second Edition*. Jena: G. Fisher.

Nagle, J. S. (1967). Wave and current orientation of shells. *Journal of Sedimentary Petrology*, **37**, 1124–1138.

Nebelsick, J. H. (1992). The northern bay of Safaga (Red Sea, Egypt): An actuopaläontological approach, III distribution of echinoids. *Beiträge zut Paläontologie von Österreich*, **17**, 5–79

Nebelsick, J. H. (1995a). Actuopalaeontological investigations of echinoids: The potential for taphonomic interpretations. In R. Emson, A. Smith & A. Campbell, eds., *Echinoderm Research, 1995*, Rotterdam: Balkema Press, pp. 209–214.

Nebelsick, J. H. (1995b). Uses and limitations of actuopalaeontological investigations on echinoids. *Geobios*, **18**, 329–336.

Nebelsick, J. H. (1995c). Comparative taphonomy of Clypeasteroids. *Ecologae Geologicue Helvetiae* **88**, 685–693.

Nebelsick, J. H. (1996). Biodiversity of shallow-water Red Sea echinoids: implications for the fossil record. *Journal of the Marine Biological Association. U.K.* **76**, 185–194.

Nebelsick, J. H. (2008). Taphonomy of the irregular echinoid *Clypeaster humilis* from the Red Sea: Implications for taxonomic resolution along taphonomic gradients. In W. I. Ausich & G. D. Webster, eds., *Echinoderm Paleobiology*. Bloomington: Indiana University Press, pp. 115–128.

Nebelsick, J. H., Dynowski, J. F., Grossmann, J. N., & Tötzke, C. (2015). Echinoderms: Hierarchically organized light weight skeletons. In C. Hamm, ed., *Evolution of Lightweight Structures: Analyses and Technical Applications, Biologically-Inspired Systems*, Vol. 6, London: Springer-Verlag, 141–156. DOI 10.1007/978–017-9398–8_8. ISBN-10: 9401793972.

Nebelsick, J. H., & Kampfer, S. (1994). Taphonomy of *Cypeaster humilis* and *Echinodiscus auritus* (Echinoidea, Clypeateroide) from the Red Sea. In B. David, A. Guille, J.-P. Feral, and M. Roux, eds., *Echinoderms Through Time*, Rotterdam: Balkema, pp. 803–808.

Nebelsick, J. H., & Kroh, A. (1999). Palaeoecology and taphonomy of Parascutella bed from the lower Miocene of the Eastern Desert, Egypt. In M. D. Candia Carnevali & F. Bonasoro, eds., *Echinoderm Research 1998*. Rotterdam: A.A. Balkema Press, p.353.

Nebelsick, J. H., & Mancosu, A. (2021). *The taphonomy of echinoids: skeletal morphologies, environmental factors, and preservational pathways*. Element in preparation.

Newell, N. D., Imbie, J., Purdy, E. G., & Thurber, D. L. (1959). Organism communities and bottom facies, Great Bahamas Bank. *Bulletin of the American Museum of Natural History*, **117**, 177–228.

Oji, T., & Amemiya, S. (1998). Survival of crinoid stalk fragments and its taphonomic implications. *Paleontological Research*, **2**, 67–70.

Okulitch, V. J., & Tovell, W. M. (1941). A crinoidal marking in the Dundas Formation at Toronto. *Journal of Paleontology*, **15**, 89.

O'Malley, C. E., Ausich, W. I., & Chin. Y-P. (2008). Crinoid biomarkers (Borden Group, Mississippian): Implications for phylogeny. In W. I. Ausich and

G. D. Webster, eds., *Echinoderm Paleobiology*, Bloomington: Indiana University Press, pp. 290–306.

O'Malley, C. E., Ausich, W. I., & Chin. Y-P. (2013). Isolation and characterization of the earliest taxon-specific organic molecules (Mississippian, Crinoidea). *Geology*, **41**, 347–350. (doi:10.1130/G33792.1)

O'Malley, C. E., Ausich, W. I., & Chin. Y-P. (2016). Deep echinoderm phylogeny preserved in organic molecules from Paleozoic fossils. *Geology*, **4**, 379–382. [doi:10.1130/G37761.1]

Parsley, R. (2009). Morphology, ontogeny, and heterochrony in Lower and Middle Cambrian gogiids (Eocrinoidea, Echinodermata) from Guizhou Province, China. *Palaeontological Journal*, **43**, 1406–1414.

Parsley, R. L., & Zhou, Y. (2006). Long stalked eocrinoids in the basal Middle Cambrian Kaili Biota, Taijiang County, Guizhou Province, China. *Journal of Paleontology*, **80**, 1058–1071.

Pawson, D. L. (1980). Holothurians. In T. W. Broadhead & J. A. Waters, eds., *Echinoderm Notes for a Short Course*. Knoxville: University of Tennessee Studies in Geology, 3, 175–189.

Purdy, E. G. (1963). Recent calcium carbonate facies on the Great Bahamas Bank, 2, sedimentary facies. *Journal of Geology*, **71**, 472–497.

Régis, M. B. (1977). Organisation microstructurale du stéréome de l'Echinoïde *Paracentrotus lifidus* Lamarck et ses éventuelles incidences physiologiques. *Comptes Rendus de l'Académie des Sciences Paris, Séries D*, **285**, 189–192.

Reid, M., Bordy, E. M., & Taylor, W. (2015). Taphonomy and sedimentology of an echinoderm obrution bed in the Lower Devonian Voorstehoek Formation (Bokkeveld Group, Cape Supergroup) of South Africa. *Journal of African Earth Sciences*, **110**, 135–149.

Rhenberg, E. C., Ausich, W. I., & Meyer, D. L. (2016). Actinocrinitidae from the Lower Mississippian Fort Payne Formation of Kentucky and Alabama. *Journal of Paleontology*, **90**,1148–1159. http//dx.doi.org/10.1017/jpa.2016.85

Riddle, S. W., Wulff, J. I. & Ausich, W. I. (1988). Biomechanics and stereomic microstructure of the *Gilbertsocrinus tuberosus* column. In R. D. Burke, P. V. Mladenov, P. Lambert, and R. L. Parsley, eds., *Echinoderm Biology*. Rotterdam: A.A. Balkema, pp. 641–648.

Rosenkranz, D. (1971). Zur sedimentology und Okölogie von Echinoderm-Lagerstätten. *Neues Jahrbuch für Geologie und Paläontologie, Abhandlungen*, **138**, 221–258.

Rousseau, J., Gale, A. S., & Thuy, B. (2018). New articulated asteroids (Echinodermata, Asteroidea) and ophiuroids (Echinodermata, Ophiuroidea) from the Late Jurassic (Volgian/Tithian) of central Spitsbergen. *European Journal of Taxonomy*, **411**, 1–6.

Roux, M. (1970). Introduction à l'etude des microstructures des tiges de crinöids. *Geobios*, **3**, 79–98.

Roux, M. (1974a). Les principaux modes d'articulation des ossicules du squelete des Crinöides pédonculés actuels, Observations microstructurales et consequences pour l'interprétation des fossils. *Compte Rendu de l'Academie des Sciences, Paris*, **278**, 2015–2018.

Roux, M. (1974b). Observations au microscope électronique à bakayage de quelques articulations entre les ossicules de sequelette des Crinöides pédonculés actuels (Bathycrinidae et Isocrinina). *Travaux du Labroratoire de Paléontologie, Orsay*, 10 p.

Roux, M. (1975). Microstructural analysis of the crinoid stem. *University of Kansas Paleontological Contributions, Paper*, **75**, 1–7.

Sadler, M., & Lewis, R. D. (1996). Actualistic studies of taphonomy and ichnology the of irregular echinoid *Meoma verntricosa* at San Salvador, Bahamas. *Geological Society of America Abstracts with Programs*, **28**, 293–294.

Savarese, M., Dodd, J. R., & Lane, N. G. (1997). Taphonomic and sedimentologic implications of crinoid intraskeletal porosity. *Lethaia*, **29**, 141–156.

Schäfer, W. (1972). *Ecology and Paleoecology of Marine Environments*. Chicago: University of Chicago Press.

Schneider, C. L., Sprinkle, J., & Ryder, D. (2005). Pennsylvanian (Late Carboniferous) echinoids from the Winchell Formation, North-Central Texas, USA. *Journal of Paleontology*, **79**, 745–762.

Schumacher, G. A. (1986). Storm processes and crinoid preservation. *Abstracts, Fourth North American Paleontological Convention, Boulder, 12–15 August*, p. A41.

Schwarzacher, W. (1961). Petrology and structure of some Loer Carboniferous reefs in northwestern Ireland. *Journal of Sedimentary Petrology*, **45**, 481–503.

Schwarzacher, W. (1963). Orientation of crinoid by current action. *Journal of Sedimentary Geology*, **33**, 580–586.

Seilacher, A. (1960). Strömumgsanzeichen in Hunsrückshiefer Notizblatt des Hessischen. *Landesant für Bodenforschung zu Wiesbaden*, **88**, 88–106.

Seilacher, A. (1968). Origin and diagenesis of the Oriskany Sandstone (Lower Devonian, Appalachians) as reflected in the fossil shells. In B. Müller & G. M. Friedman, eds., *Recent Developments in Sedimentary Geology in Central Europe*, New York: Springer-Verlag, pp. 175–185.

Seilacher, A. (1979). Constructional morphology of sand dollars. *Paleobiology*, **5**, 1–20.

Sevastopulo, G. D., & Keegan, J. B. (1980). A technique for revealing the stereom structure of fossil crinoids. *Palaeontology*, **23**, 749–756.

Shroat-Lewis, R. A., McKinney, M. L., Brett, C. E., Meyer, D. L., & Sumrall, C. D. (2011). Paleoecological assessment of an edrioasteroid (Echinodermata)-encrusted hardground from the Upper Ordovician (Maysvillian) Bellevue Member, Maysville, Kentucky. *PALAIOS*, **26**, 470–483.

Shroat-Lewis, R. A., Sumrall, C. D., McKinney, M. L., & Meyer, D. L. (2014). A paleoecological comparison of two edrioasteroid (Echinodermata) encrusted pavements from the Upper Ordovician Correyville Formation of Florence, Kentucky and the Miamitown Shale of Sharonville, Ohio, U.S.A. *PALAIOS*, **29**, 154–169.

Shroat-Lewis, R. A., Greenwood, E. N., & Sumrall, C. D. (2019). Paleoecological analysis of edrioasteroid (Echinodermata) encrusted slabs from the Chesterian (Upper Mississippian) Kinkaid Limestone of southern Illinois. *PALAIOS*, **34**, 146–158.

Smith, A. B. (1980). Stereom microstructure of echinoid tests. *Special Papers in Palaeontology*, **25**, 1–81.

Smith, A. B. (1984). *Echinoid Paleobiology*. London:George Allen and Unwin.

Smith, A. B., & Gallemí, J. (1991). Middle Triassic holothurians from northern Spain. *Palaeontology*, **34**, 49–76.

Smith, A. B., & Paul, C. R. C. (1982). Revision of the class Cyclocystoidea (Echinodermata). *Philosophical Transactions of the Royal Society of London, B, Biological Series*, **296**, 577–684.

Smith, A. B., & Rader, W. L. (2009). Echinoid diversity, preservation potential and sequence stratigraphic cycles in the Glen Rose Formation (early Albian, Early Cretaceous), Texas, USA. *Palaeobiodiversity and Palaeoenvironments*, **89**, 7–52.

Smith, A. B., Reich, M., & Zamora, A. (2009). Morphology and ecological setting of the basal echinoid genus *Rhenechinus* from the early Devonian of Spain. *Acta Palaeontologica Polonica*, **58**, 751–762.

Smosma, R. (1988). Paleogeographic reconstruction of the Lower Devonian Helderberg Group in the Appalachian Basin. In N. J. McMillan, A. F. Embry & D. J. Glass, eds., *Devonian of the World, Proceedings of the Second International Symposium on the Devonian of the World, Calgary, Canada*, **1**, 265–275. Canadian Society of Petroleum Geologists.

Spencer, W. K., & Wright, C. W. (1966). Asterozoans. In R. C. Moore, ed., *Treatise on Invertebrate Paleontology, Part V, Echinodermata 3*. Lawrence, KS, Boulder, CO: University of Kansas Paleontological Institute and Geological Society of America, pp. U4–U107.)

Sprinkle, J. (1973). Morphology and evolution of blastozoan echinoderms. *Harvard Museum of Comparative Zoology Special Publication*, 283 p.

Sprinkle, J. (1982). Echinoderm zones and faunas of the Bromide Formation (Middle Ordovician) of Oklahoma. *University of Kansas Paleontological Contributions Monograph*, **1**, 46–56.

Sprinkle, J., and Guensburg, T. E. (1995). Origin of echinoderms in the Paleozoic Evolutionary Fauna: The role of substrates. *PALAIOS*, 10, 437–453.

Sprinkle, J., & Gutschick, R. C. (1967). *Costaloblastus*, a channel fill blastoids from the Sappington Formation of Montana. *Journal of Paleontology*, **41**, 385–402.

Sroka, S. D. (1988). Preliminary studies on a complete fossil holothurian from the Middle Pennsylvanian Francis Shale of Illinois. In R. D. Burke, P. V. Mladenov, P. Lambert, and R. L. Parsley, eds., *Echinoderm Biology, Proceedings of the Sixth International Echinoderm Conference, Victoria, British Columbia. 23–28 August, 1987*. Rotterdam: Balkema Press, pp. 159–160.

Sroka, S. D., & Blake, D. B. (1997). Echinodermata. In C. W. Shabica, and A. A. Hay, eds., *Richardson's Guide to the Fossil Fauna of Mazon Creek*. Chicago, IL: Northeastern University Press, pp. 223–225.

Stevenson, A., Gahn, F. J., Baumiller, T. K., & Sevastopulo, G. D. (2017). Predation on feather stars by regular echinoids as evidenced by laboratory and field observations and its paleobiological implications. *Paleobiology*, **43**, 274–285.

Stolarski, J., Gorzelak, P., Mazur, M., Marrocchi, Y., & Meibon, A. (2009). Nanostructural and geochemical features of the Jurassic isocrinids columnal ossicles. *Acta Palaeontological Polonica*, **54**, 69–75.

Strimple, H. L., & Moore, R. C. (1971). Crinoids from the LaSalle Limestone (Pennsylvanian) Illinois. *University of Kansas Paleontological Institute, Echinodermata Article* **11**, 48 p.

Sumrall, C. D. (2000). The biologic implications of an edrioasteroid attached to a pleurocystitid rhombiferan. *Journal of Paleontology*, **84**, 356–359.

Sumrall, C. D. (2001). Paleoecology and taphonomy of two new edrioasteroids from a Mississippian hardground in Kentucky. *Journal of Paleontology*, **75**, 136–146

Sumrall, C. D. (2010). The systematics of a new upper Ordovician edrioasteroid pavement from northern Kentucky. *Journal of Paleontology*, **84**, 783–794.

Sumrall, C. D., Brett, C. E., Work, P. T., & Meyer, D. L. (2001). Taphonomy and paleoecology of an edrioasteroid encrusted hardground in the Bellevue Formation at Maysville, Kentucky. In T. J. Algeo & C. E. Brett, eds., *Sequence, Cycle, and Event Stratigraphy of Upper Ordovician and Silurian*

Strata of the Cincinnati Arch Region. Kentucky Geological Survey, Kentucky Guidebook Series **12**, 1, 123–131.

Sumrall, C. D., Sprinkle, J., & Bonem, R. M. (2006). An edrioasteroid-dominated echinoderm assemblage from a Lower Pennsylvanian marine conglomerate in Oklahoma. *Journal of Paleontology*, **80**, 229–244.

Taylor, W. L., & Brett, C. E. (1996). Taphonomy and paleoecology of echinoderm *Lagerstätten* from the Silurian (Wenlockian) Rochester Shale. *PALAIOS*, **11**, 118–140.

Telford M. (1985a). Domes, arches and urchins: the skeletal architecture of echinoids (Echinodermata). *Zoomorphology*, **105**, 114–124.

Telford M. (1985b). Structural analysis of the test of *Echinocyamus pusillus* (O. F. Müller). In B. F. Keegan and B. D. S. O'Conner, eds., *Proceedings of the Fifth International Echinoderm Conference*. Rotterdam: Balkema, pp. 353–360.

Thompka, J. R., Lewis, R.D., Mosher, D., Pabian, R. K., & Holterhoff, P. F. (2011). Genus-level taphonomic variation within cladid crinoids from the Upper Pennsylvanian Barnsdall Formation, northeastern Oklahoma. *PALAIOS*, **26**, 377–389.

Tetreault, D. K. (1995). An unusual Silurian arthropod/echinoderm dominated soft-bodied fauna from the Eramosa Member (Ludlow) of the Guelph Formation, southern Bruce Peninsula, Ontario, Canada. *Geological Society of America Abstracts with Programs*, **27**, A–114.

Ubaghs, G. (1963). *Rhopalocystis detombsei* n. gen., n. sp. Eocrinoïde de l'Ordovicien inférieur (Trémadocien supériur de Sud marocain. *Notes du Service Géologique du Marocain*, **23**, 25–45.

Veitch M. A., Messing, C. G., & Baumiller, T. K. (2015). Contractile connective tissue (CCT) in the stalk of the bourgueticrinid crinoid, *Democrinus*: functional, ecological, and evolutionary implications. Geological Society of America Abstracts with Programs, **47(7)**, 855.

Wachsmuth, C., & Springer, F. (1880–1886). Revision of the Palaeocrinoidea. Proceedings of the Academy of Natural Sciences of Philadelphia Pt. I. The families Ichthyocrinidae and Cyathocrinidae (1880), pp. 226–378, (separate repaged pp. 1–153). Pt. II. Family Sphaeroidocrinidae, with the sub-families Platycrinidae, Rhodocrinidae, and Actinocrinidae (1881), pp. 177–411, (separate repaged, pp. 1–237). Pt. III, Sec. 1. Discussion of the classification and relations of the brachiate crinoids, and conclusion of the generic descriptions (1885), pp. 225–364 (separate repaged, pp. 1–138). Pt. III, Sec. 2. Discussion of the classification and relations of the brachiate crinoids, and conclusion of the generic descriptions (1886), pp. 64–226 (separate repaged to continue with section 1, pp. 139–302).

Waddington, J. B. (1980). A soft substrata community with edrioasteroids from the Verulum Formation (Middle Ordovician) at Gambridge, Ontario. *Canadian Journal of Earth Sciences*, **17**, 674–749.

Weber, J. N. (1969). The incorporation of magnesium into the skeletal calcite of echinoderms. *American Journal of Science*, **267**, 537–566.

Welch, J. R. (1984). The asteroid *Lepidasterella montanaensis* n. sp., from the upper Mississippian Bear Gulch Formation of Montana. *Journal of Paleontology*, **58**, 843–851.

Wilson, J. L. (1975). *Carbonate Facies in Geologic History*. New York: Springer-Verlag, 471 p.

Witzke, B. J., Tassier-Surine, S. A., Anderson, R. R., Bunker, B. J., & Artz, J. A. (2002). Pleistocene, Mississippian, and Devonian Stratigraphy of the Burlington, Iowa, area. *Iowa Geological Survey Guidebook*, **23**, 23–51 p.

Wolkenstein, K., Głuchowski, E., Gross, J. H., & Marynowski, L. (2008). Hypericrinoid pigments in millericrinids from the lower Kimmeridgian of the Holy Cross Mountains (Poland). *PALAIOS*, **23**, 773–777.

Wolkenstein, K., Gross, J. H., Heinz, F., & Schöler, H. F. (2006). Preservation of hypericine and related polycyclic quinone pigments in fossil crinoids. *Proceedings of the Royal Society, B–Biological Sciences*, **273**, 451–456, doi:10.1098/rspb.2005.3358

Wright, D. F. (2017a). Bayesian estimation of fossil phylogenies and the evolution of early to middle Paleozoic crinoids (Echinodermata). *Journal of Paleontology*, 91, 799–814. doi: 10.1017/jpa.2016.141.

Wright, D. F. (2017b). Phenotypic innovation and adaptive constraints in the evolutionary radiation of Palaeozoic crinoids. *Scientific Reports*, 7: 13745 | DOI:10.1038/s41598-017-13979-9.

Wright, D. F., Ausich, W. I., Cole, S. R., Peter, M. E., & Rhenberg, E. C., (2017). Phylogenetic taxonomy and classification of the Crinoidea (Echinodermata): *Journal of Paleontology*, **91**, 829–846. doi 10.1917/jpa.2016.142; published online 02-22-17.

Zhao, Y., Parsley, R. L., & Peng, J. (2008). Basal middle Cambrian short-stalked eocrinoids from the Kaili Biota: Guizhou Province, China. *Journal of Paleontology*, **82**, 415–422.

Zamora, S., Gozalo, R. & Linñán, E. (2009). Middle Cambrian gogiid echinoderms from Northeastern Spain: Taxonomy, palaeoecology, and palaeogeographic implications. *Acta Palaeontologica Polonica*, **54**, 253–265.

Zittel, K. A. von. (1895). *Grundzüge der Palaeontologie (Palaeozoologie)*, 1st edit. München: R. Oldenbourg.

Acknowledgments

This short course notes Element is summary of the numerous, enthusiastic group of students of the Echinodermata, a fascinating group of organisms that spark the imagination. An attempt has been made to cite as many studies as possible, but it was impossible to list every relevant study. Several colleagues helped by discussing ideas for this Element and providing images, including L. Boucher, J.-P. Lin, W. B. Lyons, C. G. Messing, J. H. Nebelsick, C. Schneider, G. D. Sevastopulo, C. D. Sumrall, and J. Thompson. I also thank the reviewers, J. Nebelsick and G. D. Sevastopulo, who significantly improved this manuscript.

Cambridge Elements ☰

Elements of Paleontology

Editor-in-Chief
Colin D. Sumrall
University of Tennessee

About the Series
The Elements of Paleontology series is a publishing collaboration between the Paleontological Society and Cambridge University Press. The series covers the full spectrum of topics in paleontology and paleobiology, and related topics in the Earth and life sciences of interest to students and researchers of paleontology.
The Paleontological Society is an international nonprofit organization devoted exclusively to the science of paleontology: invertebrate and vertebrate paleontology, micropaleontology, and paleobotany. The Society's mission is to advance the study of the fossil record through scientific research, education, and advocacy. Its vision is to be a leading global advocate for understanding life's history and evolution. The Society has several membership categories, including regular, amateur/avocational, student, and retired. Members, representing some 40 countries, include professional paleontologists, academicians, science editors, Earth science teachers, museum specialists, undergraduate and graduate students, postdoctoral scholars, and amateur/avocational paleontologists.

Paleontological
S O C I E T Y

Cambridge Elements $\equiv$

Elements of Paleontology

Elements in the Series

Printed in the United States
By Bookmasters